The Postwar Quality
of State and Local Debt

NATIONAL BUREAU OF ECONOMIC RESEARCH
Number 94, General Series

The Postwar
Quality of
State and Local Debt

GEORGE H. HEMPEL

Washington University

National Bureau of Economic Research

NEW YORK

1971

Distributed by Columbia University Press

NEW YORK AND LONDON

Relation of the Directors to the Work and Publications of the National Bureau of Economic Research

1. The object of the National Bureau of Economic Research is to ascertain and to present to the public important economic facts and their interpretation in a scientific and impartial manner. The Board of Directors is charged with the responsibility of ensuring that the work of the National Bureau is carried on in strict conformity with this object.

2. The President of the National Bureau shall submit to the Board of Directors, or to its Executive Committee, for their formal adoption all specific proposals for research to be instituted.

3. No research report shall be published until the President shall have submitted to each member of the Board the manuscript proposed for publication, and such information as will, in his opinion and in the opinion of the author, serve to determine the suitability of the report for publication in accordance with the principles of the National Bureau. Each manuscript shall contain a summary drawing attention to the nature and treatment of the problem studied, the character of the data and their utilization in the report, and the main conclusions reached.

4. For each manuscript so submitted, a special committee of the Board shall be appointed by majority agreement of the President and Vice Presidents (or by the Executive Committee in case of inability to decide on the part of the President and Vice Presidents), consisting of three directors selected as nearly as may be one from each general division of the Board. The names of the special manuscript committee shall be stated to each Director when the manuscript is submitted to him. It shall be the duty of each member of the special manuscript committee to read the manuscript. If each member of the manuscript committee signifies his approval within thirty days of the transmittal of the manuscript, the report may be published. If at the end of that period any member of the manuscript committee withholds his approval, the President shall then notify each member of the Board, requesting approval or disapproval of publication, and thirty days additional shall be granted for this purpose. The manuscript shall then not be published unless at least a majority of the entire Board who shall have voted on the proposal within the time fixed for the receipt of votes shall have approved.

5. No manuscript may be published, though approved by each member of the special manuscript committee, until forty-five days have elapsed from the transmittal of the report in manuscript form. The interval is allowed for the receipt of any memorandum of dissent or reservation, together with a brief statement of his reasons, that any member may wish to express; and such memorandum of dissent or reservation shall be published with the manuscript if he so desires. Publication does not, however, imply that each member of the Board has read the manuscript, or that either members of the Board in general or the special committee have passed on its validity in every detail.

6. Publications of the National Bureau issued for informational purposes concerning the work of the Bureau and its staff, or issued to inform the public of activities of Bureau staff, and volumes issued as a result of various conferences involving the National Bureau shall contain a specific disclaimer noting that such publication has not passed through the normal review procedures required in this resolution. The Executive Committee of the Board is charged with review of all such publications from time to time to ensure that they do not take on the character of formal research reports of the National Bureau, requiring formal Board approval.

7. Unless otherwise determined by the Board or exempted by the terms of paragraph 6, a copy of this resolution shall be printed in each National Bureau publication.

(Resolution adopted October 25, 1926, and revised February 6, 1933, February 24, 1941, and April 20, 1968)

Contents

Contents

Tables

Charts

ACKNOWLEDGMENTS

A number of people have contributed to the development of this study. The early ideas and original data were obtained as part of the research for my doctoral dissertation supervised by C. James Pilcher at the University of Michigan. Many of the major parts of the study were completed in 1966 when I was a faculty research associate at the National Bureau of Economic Research. During this period I received numerous helpful suggestions from members of the National Bureau staff including Geoffrey H. Moore, Jack M. Guttentag, Edgar R. Fiedler, James S. Earley, Avery Cohan, F. Thomas Juster, Solomon Fabricant and Ilse Mintz.

Other groups were helpful, as well. First, several organizations were willing to provide much of the data needed for analysis in the study. These organizations included: Dun and Bradstreet, Investment Bankers Association, Moody's Investors Service, Rand and Company, The Bureau of the Census, Standard and Poor's Corporation, The Federal Deposit Insurance Corporation and *The Bond Buyer*. Second, several patient research assistants greatly aided in the gathering and analysis of the needed data. These included Guy Baughns, Mary Anne Sudol and Antonette Burger Delak of the National Bureau staff. Finally, Ross M. Trump, Joseph W. Towle and Karl A. Hill of Washington University made it possible for me to have sufficient time to complete the study.

The present study has also benefited materially from the penetrating comments and constructive suggestions of the National Bureau staff reading committee, which consisted of Ilse Mintz, James S. Earley and Edgar R. Fiedler. In the later stages several other colleagues at the National Bureau, in particular, John R. Meyer, Geoffrey H. Moore, John F. Kain and Thomas Sargent and the Board of Directors reading committee — Joseph A. Beirne, Francis M. Boddy and J. Wilson Newman — also provided some helpful suggestions.

Ruth Scheetz patiently typed the original manuscript; the charts were drawn with skill and care by H. Irving Forman, and Gnomi Gouldin provided a careful and empathic editing of the manuscript.

The Postwar Quality
of State and Local Debt

1

INTRODUCTION AND SUMMARY

The use of debt has been extremely important to economic development throughout the world. Debt has brought about opportunities for economic growth and prosperity. At the same time, it has entailed problems and risks. Attempts to measure either the beneficial or negative effects of indebtedness have been notoriously weak and inexact.

Both the creation of new indebtedness and the stock of outstanding debt instruments perform important economic functions. The creation of debt is the primary means by which funds are channeled from surplus to deficit economic units. Debt, therefore, enables deficit units to use and benefit from goods and services earlier than they would otherwise be able to. At the same time, the surplus units providing the loanable funds are encouraged to save by the interest payments they receive.

The rate of interest which deficit units pay surplus units for the use of their funds should allocate savings, and the real resources they can be used to purchase, to the most effective uses. By returning savings to the spending stream in an efficient manner, debt facilitates the mobility of capital and the continuous adjustment of economic activities through time and, therefore, encourages the steady growth of production and income. This effect tends to be continuous and self-reinforcing — increases in production and income usually lead to increased indebtedness by permitting more savings by surplus economic units and by promoting a greater willingness to borrow by deficit units.

In addition, debt instruments, as an asset, also perform important economic functions. They serve as a means of payment, as a source of liquidity or as a convenient way to store savings, or any combination of the three, while at the same time earning a return roughly commensurate with risk.

The vital role that debt assumes in a highly developed market economy does not negate the problems and dangers which debt may present to the economy. Inadequate growth of debt may lead to retarded economic growth, inefficiencies in resource allocation and a low supply of liquid assets. The opposite extreme is no less undesirable. Excessive amounts of indebtedness may cause the downfall of numerous economic units and, at least temporarily, lead to some misallocations of resources. Debt payment problems resulting from debt excesses may contribute to cyclical instability either by helping to initiate a contraction in business activity or by prolonging and intensifying an economic depression.[1] Conversely, too rapid an increase in some forms of debt may lead to harmful inflation. Even if an appropriate balance of debt issued and outstanding is attained, there is the additional problem of achieving a balance in the structure and composition of debt.

The problems and dangers associated with debt, and the fact that they have not been thoroughly studied before, encouraged the National Bureau of Economic Research to undertake a quality of credit program. This study is one part of this extensive program.[2]

Purpose of the Study

One type of debt, state and local debt, is analyzed in this study. Since the end of World War II, outstanding state and local indebtedness has grown at a faster rate than any of the other principal forms of marketable debt instruments. The increase in state and local indebtedness has clearly contributed to the large growth in state and local services and, consequently, to over-all economic progress during the postwar period. No substantive studies, however, have examined the effects of this growth on the quality of state and local debt. Perhaps state and local governments have still not borrowed as much as they could productively and safely use; that is, perhaps the quality may still be too high. On the other hand, it is also possible that excessive amounts of state and local indebtedness have been issued relative to the resources available for meeting debt service payments. Such excesses, particularly if accompanied by excessive indebtedness in other sectors, might lead to intensified cyclical swings in the economy or to inflationary pressures. There might also be serious problems for the state and local sector, such as poor

---

[1]See Geoffrey H. Moore, "The Quality of Credit in Boom and Depression," *The Journal of Finance,* XI, May 1956, pp. 288-300; Arthur F. Burns and Wesley C. Mitchell, *Measuring Business Cycles,* Studies in Business Cycles 2, New York, NBER, 1946, pp. 458-464; and Philip A. Klein and Geoffrey H. Moore, *The Quality of Consumer Instalment Credit,* New York, NBER, 1967, pp. 138-173.

[2]Published studies in the quality of credit program include: Albert M. Wojnilower, *The Quality of Bank Loans: A Study of Bank Examination Records,* New York, NBER, 1962; Martin H. Seiden, *The Quality of Trade Credit,* New York, NBER, 1964; Thomas R. Atkinson, *Trends in Corporate Bond Quality,* New York, NBER, 1967; and Moore and Klein, *ibid.*

allocation of resources, inadequate growth of needed state and local services or loss of local financial control. The primary purpose of this study is to define and measure the postwar quality of state and local debt. The findings of this study should be useful in evaluating the over-all effects of the rapid postwar growth in state and local debt.

Scope of the Study

Five basic tasks are undertaken in this study: (1) a clear explanation of "quality" as used in the study; (2) an examination of the past performance of state and local debt; (3) the identification of instrument and borrower characteristics which measure the prospective quality of state and local debt; (4) an examination of the levels of the significant characteristics in recent years; and (5) an analysis of some evaluations of the level of and changes in these characteristics and the economic environment in which they exist.

The concepts of credit quality and the methods used to measure the quality of state and local debt are discussed in Chapter 2. A simple formulation of the instrument and borrower characteristics which should be indicative of the quality of state and local debt is presented in this chapter.

The past payment performance of state and local debt is examined in Chapter 3. The incidence of payment difficulties, the converse of positive payment experiences, is studied since most state and local debt has been repaid as contracted. The record of payment difficulties from the first recorded default in 1839 through the mid-1960's is examined, with special emphasis placed on those periods when the magnitude of defaults and losses became so serious that many normal state and local financial practices were ineffective.

The primary purpose of Chapter 4 is to identify instrument and borrower characteristics which measure the quality of state and local debt. Two types of evidence are examined: (1) the performance of aggregate instrument and borrower characteristics in periods when the magnitude of defaults and losses was a serious problem and (2) the performance of instrument and borrower characteristics for a cross-section of individual state and local units during the major default period starting in 1929.

The performance of the pertinent aggregate instrument and borrower characteristics is examined in Chapter 5. The figures for the period since World War II are emphasized; however, when it is available, relevant information from earlier periods is used for perspective.

The postwar performance of pertinent instrument and borrower characteristics for several major classifications of state and local debt are examined in Chapter 6. The methods of classification include: geographic region, type of governmental unit and type of resources used to pay debt service charges. This analysis helps to indicate more specific areas of strength and weakness.

The evaluations of instrument and borrower characteristics and the external environment by agencies paid to rate the quality of state and local issues is presented in Chapter 7.

The money and capital markets' evaluation of the quality of state and local debt as indicated by market yield relationships is the subject matter of Chapter 8. The relationships between the yields on state and local issues and the yields on U.S. government bonds, and the relationships among the yields on state and local debt in different rating categories and on different classifications of state and local debt are studied.

Findings of the Study

The following list summarizes many of the most pertinent findings of this study.

1. Since the amount of state and local indebtedness became significant, debt payment problems occurred nearly continuously under both good and bad economic conditions. It was only in major depression periods, however, that the extent of state and local debt payment problems rose to a level that affected state and local finance in a material way. The incidence of debt payment problems generally did not appear to be significantly affected by milder cyclical declines.

2. In each of the four major depression periods in which there were serious state and local debt payment difficulties — 1837-43, 1873-79, 1893-99 and 1929-37 — the extent of such difficulties became a serious economic problem only in the later stages of the depression. This timing characteristic indicates that state and local debt payment difficulties were at least partially caused by the severe declines in wealth and income in these periods. Furthermore, it seems to support the hypothesis that state and local debt payment difficulties add to the severity of major economic declines rather than occur as a major element leading to these declines.

3. Both time series and cross-sectional analyses of historical instrument and borrower characteristics indicated that there was a pattern among these characteristics indicative of debt payment problems. The amount of debt outstanding, a surrogate for debt service charges, increased rapidly before each of the four major default periods and prior to many individual default situations. Wealth and income measures that are indicative of potential cash inflows appear to have risen less rapidly than estimated debt service charges before the major default periods and many individual default situations. These measures then declined absolutely in the economic decline immediately preceding each of the four major default periods. Cash outlays that were paid prior to debt service charges failed to decline as rapidly as cash inflows before major default periods and for many individual default situations. Finally, the

use of state and local debt for essentially private purposes and a continuing deficit in the current account preceded both major default periods and many individual default situations.

4. If it is assumed that the risk of a serious over-all economic decline has remained constant (the major factor in the external environment has not changed), aggregative instrument and borrower characteristics affecting the quality of state and local debt indicate that this quality has weakened since the end of World War II. State and local debt, and the resulting debt service charges, generally have increased moderately faster than state and local general revenues and estimated usuable cash inflows and substantially faster than the measures indicative of potential usable cash inflows. State and local tax rates have increased rapidly in this period. The increased contribution of federal financial aid to state governmental units, of state financial aid to local governmental units and new sources of revenues based on the recipient paying for the service may strengthen revenues sufficiently to offset in part the increased debt burden. On the other hand, increased reliance by state and local units on cyclically vulnerable revenue sources and decreased flexibility in applying many state and local revenues because of earmarking and revenue declination would seem to call for greater rather than lesser coverage of debt service charges. The increased downward inelasticity of state and local expenditures also contributed to the relative decline in the quality of state and local debt. The evidence on financial prudence and willingness to pay was mixed. Prudent debt retirement practices and fewer deficits in state and local current accounts are indicative of good financial management; however, the increasing use of state and local debt to build private industrial facilities and the increased amount of indebtedness issued without voter approval are causes for concern.

5. Comparing the level of and changes in aggregate instrument and borrower characteristics in the mid-1960's with similar available measures for the late 1920's indicated that state and local units were more vulnerable to debt payment problems in the later period. As in finding 4, this higher vulnerability is based on the assumption that the risks of an over-all economic decline were the same in both periods.[3]

6. Instrument and borrower characteristics for selected classifications of state and local debt were also examined. The characteristics of state and local debt classified by type of governmental unit showed that incorporated municipalities and special districts had much higher debt burdens than other state

[3]The postwar weakening in the relative quality of state and local debt does not necessarily mean a net economic loss to society. The debt has provided certain services which have benefited the area. These benefits should be weighed against the absolute vulnerability to loss of state and local debt. Such a direct comparison is not feasible at the present time.

and local units. Instruments and borrower characteristics for state and local units in statewide geographic regions demonstrated that some states had much heavier debt burdens; however, these states were spread throughout the United States and seemed to change over time. The type of resources used to pay debt service charges proved to be the most fruitful classification in analyzing the over-all quality of state and local debt. Federally guaranteed debt has remained a constant proportion of all state and local debt over the postwar period. Short-term state and local debt has increased rapidly in the postwar period; however, so have state and local liquid assets and other measures of the ability to repay such debt. By far the most rapid relative and absolute increase in state and local debt was in the limited liability obligation. While cash flow coverage of the service charges on such indebtedness has improved moderately in the last decade, this increase may weaken the over-all quality of state and local debt. The security behind most limited liability obligations is generally weaker than full faith and credit debt. Furthermore, since all revenues from the pledged source are usually restricted to one specific project or purpose, unrestricted revenues may cover the service charges on general obligations less than before the rapid postwar growth in limited liability obligations. Unfortunately, no data on aggregate unrestricted revenues are available at the present time.

7. Most economists feel that the probability of a serious over-all economic decline has decreased. There is no consensus on the magnitude of this decrease. However, if a serious over-all economic decline should occur, another period of widespread payment difficulties in state and local debt is likely to follow, according to our findings.

8. Aggregations of agency quality ratings and market yield relationships were used to appraise the significance of instrument and borrower characteristics and to assess changes in the external environment (particularly, the possibility of a serious over-all economic decline). The rating agencies, buyers and potential buyers seem to analyze the same instrument and borrower characteristics examined in this study. In reaching a final decision, they obviously also estimated the probablity of a serious over-all economic decline. Both agency ratings and market yield relationships indicated that the quality of state and local debt was at least as high in the mid-1960's as in the early postwar years. This conclusion would seem to indicate further that these agencies and the money and capital markets felt the weakening in instrument and borrower characteristics was at least offset by the decrease in the probability of a serious economic decline.

9. Agency ratings and market yield relationships also helped to identify sectors of state and local debt which would be more likely to face payment problems. Both agency ratings and the money and capital markets evaluated the average quality of limited liability obligations as slightly below that of general obligations. The average quality of toll road revenue bonds and industrial aid revenue bonds appeared particularly weak.

2

MEASURING CREDIT QUALITY

One of the major problems in studying the quality of any group of credit instruments is understanding what is meant by "credit quality" or simply "quality." These terms have been used and interpreted in a number of ways. Quality has been used to describe the payment record of credit instruments. It has been expressed as various measures of the ability and willingness to pay and is assumed to be indicative of future payment performance. Market yield relationships have been construed as credit quality. Credit quality has also been interpreted in a social welfare context, e.g., the social welfare obtained from credit financing is compared with the past or predictive payment performance of the credit instruments.

Methods Used to Measure Credit Quality

In order to eliminate some of the confusion resulting from varied uses and interpretations of credit quality, two clearly described methods of measuring credit quality are used in this study. *Ex post quality* is a method comparing the actual incidence of payment of interest and principal with that promised for the credit instruments being studied. Defined in this manner, ex post quality can be measured only after bond principal and interest become due, and it may take long periods of time thereafter to determine if there are permanent losses. Ex post quality is usually referred to as past or realized payment performance in this study.

Ex ante quality (generally referred to as prospective quality or simply as quality) is defined as the prospective incidence of payment of principal and interest when they become due. Because ex ante quality purports to measure the prospective incidence of future events, it must be formulated as a probability measure. Defined in this manner, the prospective quality of any grouping of credit instruments is based primarily on two major determinants: (1)

the characteristics of the instrument and the borrower and (2) the future environment that the issues are likely to face.

The credit instrument characteristics include the specific security pledged, the maturity, the legality of the obligations, the provisions for sinking funds, etc. The characteristics of the borrower are indicative of his ability and willingness to pay the debt service charges, and include measures such as the borrower's wealth, cash inflows and financial management abilities.

Instrument and borrower characteristics, per se, do not take account of the future external environment in which the indebtedness will exist. External factors, such as the economic conditions during the life of the instrument, clearly affect the prospective incidence of payment difficulties. The future external environment, therefore, must be included as a determinant of credit quality. Unfortunately, the future environment can not be measured precisely at the present time.

Even if one assumes an average or normal future external environment, he still faces the formidable task of determining which instrument and borrower characteristics will affect future payment performance. Also, how much weight should each characteristic be assigned? These decisions are affected by the characteristics available and their significance in the past.

Instrument and borrower characteristics are evaluated by several groups: analysts and economists studying the quality of credit instruments, investment services paid to rate this quality, lenders supplying funds, purchasers and potential purchasers of marketable instruments. The evaluation by rating services and the money and capital markets combine their assessment of instrument and borrower characteristics with that of the future external environment. An individual assessing quality can evaluate the significance of instrument and borrower characteristics, assuming an average or normal economic environment, then add his evaluations about the future external environment.

Using the two restricted methods of measuring quality defined above, the measurement of ex post or ex ante quality is separated from the effects of the level of and changes in such quality. Changes in the realized payment experience or in the probability of payment are assumed to have no direct connotation, per se, for economic activity. For example, if prospective quality has weakened (less probability of payment in full at the time promised), it does not necessarily follow that this alone has dangerous or bad implications for over-all economic activity. Also, the concepts of quality, as defined above, do not include a normative judgment of the social benefits or costs resulting from the use of credit. For example, if the probability of meeting all debt payments when they are due has risen, quality is strengthened, even though the economy may have been hurt by the lack of credit-financed improvements.

Measurement of the Quality of State and Local Debt

State and local debt is defined as all long-term credit obligations and all interest-bearing short-term credit obligations of state and local governments and their agencies. Defined in this manner, state and local debt includes judgments, mortgages and revenue bonds, as well as general obligation bonds, notes and interest-bearing warrants. Excluded under the definition are interfund obligations, noninterest-bearing short-term obligations (e.g., trade credit), amounts owed in a trust or agency capacity, advances and contingent loans from other governments and rights of individuals to benefit from employee-retirement funds.

Even the two strictly defined methods of measuring quality described above are difficult to apply to state and local debt. Practical and conceptual problems limit the value of past payment data. Historical records are incomplete. Both borrowers and lenders may find it advantageous to conceal non-payment of bond principal and interest. Permanent losses are difficult or impossible to estimate accurately. There are several methods of measuring the dollar amount in default and these different methods are often confused in literature on the subject. Conceptually, past payment performance would seem to indicate that all state and local debt on which principal and interest were paid when due were of similar and highest ex post quality. In a strict ex post sense this is correct. However, issuers who had to pay much higher interest costs, holders who were forced to sell the bonds they held at a loss (due to lower prospective quality rather than interest rate changes) and holders who were forced to accept a refunding issue, often at a lower return, would probably disagree with the high ex post quality designation given to all such bonds.

Because of the greater availability of data on the number and dollar amount of state and local debt in default, these measures are generally used to indicate past payment performance in this study. Permanent dollar losses of principal and interest from defaults are used whenever adequate information is available. Forced refundings and fundings to avoid defaults are used in some cross-sectional analyses; however, no aggregative time series data are available. This lack of aggregate data is unfortunate, since such fundings and refundings may be an important form of state and local debt payment difficulties. Substantially lower debt prices and higher interest costs (due to lower probability that responsible state and local units could meet their debt service payments) are not used as a measure of past payment performance in this study.

The measurement of prospective quality is even more difficult. Conceptually, if sufficient information on instrument characteristics, borrower characteristics and the external environment were available, it would be possible to construct probability distributions for the payment of bond principal and interest. In the case of state and local debt, it is not feasible at this time to construct probability distributions for individual issues or for the state and local segment of the economy for several reasons. Few borrower characteristics are directly associated with the ability to meet debt service payments. For example, proxies, such as the wealth and income of taxpayers in the government unit, must often be used instead of direct measures and may vary greatly depending on who assigns valuations to them. Information on some of the borrower characteristics which can be quantified is not available at the present time. Nor can the effects of the future environment in which state and local debt exists be measured precisely at the present time.

In spite of these problems, it is feasible to roughly estimate how the over-all prospective quality of state and local debt has changed during the postwar period. This objective can be accomplished by selecting measurable instrument and borrower characteristics which seem related in a significant way to the debt quality. The degree to which these selected characteristics affect quality can be estimated by observing their significance in the past and their evaluation by the money and capital markets and investment services that rate state and local bonds. The environment that state and local indebtedness is likely to face must then be evaluated. Some rough ideas may be obtained from evaluations of the quality of such debt by rating agencies and by the money and capital markets.

A Conceptual Model

In order to classify instrument and borrower characteristics into meaningful categories for analysis, a simple conceptual model indicating prospective quality is formulated. This model is used as a framework in examining the influence of instrument and borrower characteristics upon past payment performance. In addition, it acts as a framework in measuring the effect of the characteristics on prospective quality and in pointing out those characteristics used by rating agencies and the money and capital markets.

The conceptual model of instrument and borrower characteristics formulated for use in this study is based on a general credit principle that should be applicable for any type of debt instrument. Financial prudence and willingness to pay on the part of the borrower are assumed. The amount of debt service charges which can successfully be met depends on the minimum cash flow that can be used to pay these charges during the life of the debt. This general credit principle can be transformed into a model with four variables (or groupings of variables for a similar purpose): (1) the debt service charges that must be paid; (2) the expected over-all cash inflows during the life of the debt; (3) the expected cash expenditures or outflows that will be paid prior to debt service charges during the life of the debt; and (4) the variables that measure the validity of the assumption of financial prudence and willingness to pay.

The relationships between the variables measuring the prospective quality of state and local debt seem reasonably clear. Assuming financial prudence and willingness to pay, an individual issue should be paid when due as long as debt service charges are covered by the minimum expected difference between over-all cash inflows and prior cash outflows.[1] The minimum expected difference between over-all cash inflows and prior cash outflows is usually estimated by examining the present level of this cash flow difference and its largest expected decline. Because of uncertainties about the size and duration of the largest expected decline in the cash flow difference, the prospective quality of an issue is generally expressed in terms of the probability of the debt service charges being paid when due. Doubts as to the financial prudence or willingness to pay of the borrower would lower this probability.

Measuring the level of and movements in the prospective quality of total state and local debt within the framework of this model is difficult. There are two possible approaches. Estimate the quality of individual issues for a representative sample of issues at several points of time. Or, examine the averages (and dispersion when possible) of total debt service charges, over-all cash inflows, over-all prior cash outflows, etc., at several points of time. Both of these approaches involve technical problems and would include probability estimates for the expected decline in cash coverage. Nevertheless, the measurement of the prospective quality of state and local debt would seem to be a quantifiable problem.

The inexact nature of both the expected cash inflows during the period of the indebtedness and the expected cash outflows to be paid prior to debt service costs further complicates the measurement of prospective quality. The expected cash inflows are a function of future level of wealth and income in the government unit and the amount that members of the unit will be willing to pay in the form of taxes or payments for services. The situation is further complicated by questions such as which wealth and income measures are really pertinent in determining future taxpaying ability and how much additional debt financing is available as a potential short-run source of cash. Expected cash expenditures having priority over debt service costs depend on such variables as the future demand for state and local services (and its elasticity) and cash expenditures if wealth and income decline. Because of the

[1]Proceeds from the sale of liquid assets and from additional debt financing should be included as potential short-term sources of over-all cash inflows when the minimum expected cash difference is computed.

inexact nature of cash inflows and outflows, proxies must be used for these key measures.

There are several other serious difficulties which limit the exact measurement of the prospective quality of state and local debt. For example, no aggregate state and local debt service charge figures are available at this time. There is considerable controversy over the variables to use in measuring prudence and willingness to pay. Because of the vagueness in measuring the prospective quality of state and local debt, it seems probable that different judges select and weigh the available instrument and borrower characteristics in different ways, even within a similar conceptual model. For this reason it seems profitable to present not only the authors' evaluation of such characteristics but also the evaluations used by rating agencies and the money and capital markets.

In the following two chapters the past payment performance of state and local debt is studied and the historical record of instrument and borrower characteristics as indicators of debt payment difficulties is examined.

3

PAST PAYMENT PERFORMANCE

A careful examination of the debt payment performance of state and local governmental units helps to identify the instrument and borrower characteristics which have led to payment difficulties in the past and which may be indicative of future difficulties. This study examines only the incidence and causes of payment difficulties, the converse of positive payment experiences, since most state and local debt is repaid as contracted. Three measures of absolute past payment performance are employed: (1) the number of state and local units with debt in default, (2) the dollar amount of state and local debt in default and (3) permanent dollar losses of principal and interest. Wherever possible, these three measures are compared with the appropriate number of issues or the dollar amount of state and local debt outstanding to provide relative measures of past performance which are comparable over time.[1]

A default is defined as the failure to pay a loan's interest or principal or both when due. In order to eliminate very temporary or technical defaults, the study arbitrarily excludes defaults of less than one month's duration. The number of state and local units with debt in default is consistent with this definition throughout the study. The dollar amount in default is more diffi-

[1] A detailed description of state and local debt payment difficulties from 1837 through 1963 appears in George H. Hempel, "Postwar Quality of Municipal Bonds," unpublished Ph.D. dissertation of the University of Michigan, 1964, pp. 84-161. The primary sources for the information on debt payment difficulties in this dissertation and additional details on many additional individual default situations appear in: (1) Carl H. Chatters, ed., *Municipal Debt Defaults: Their Prevention and Adjustment,* Chicago, Municipal Financial Officers Association, 1933; (2) Benjamin U. Ratchford, *American State Debts,* Durham, N.C., 1941; (3) Albert M. Hillhouse, *Municipal Bonds: A Century of Experience,* New York, 1936; (4) William A. Raymond, *State and Municipal Bonds,* New York, 1932; and (5) William A. Scott, *Repudiation of State Indebtedness,* New York, 1893.

cult to determine. At least three definitions of the dollar amount in default
have been used rather frequently in the past. First, some sources have used
the total debt of the defaulting governmental unit as the amount in default.
Another source defines it as the total of overdue interest, overdue principal
and any additional principal upon which interest is overdue. The third definition limits it to the overdue interest and principal.[2] The second and third
definitions are complicated by the fact that to be conceptually correct they
should include the accrued interest on all defaulted payments. This study uses
all three definitions when the data are available, and the definition that is
employed is carefully labeled.

Permanent losses clearly include repudiations — long continued defaults
for which the governmental units openly plan to evade payments — and
default situations in which interest or principal or both have been scaled
down. In addition, there are several other amounts which might be included
as losses: interest payments on repudiated municipal debts, accrued interest
on unpaid interest and forced refunding operations at lower interest costs.
These amounts are not included because no reasonably accurate figures are
available.

Payment Difficulties Through 1929

Chart 1 shows the number of state and local units with debt default by the
year in which the default was first reported from 1839 (when Mobile, Alabama, recorded the first default) through 1929. The primary reason that no
defaults on state and local indebtedness were recorded prior to 1839 was
probably the antagonism toward any economic unit going into debt during
the early years of American independence. In 1790, the United States government assumed all outstanding state indebtedness. Little, if any, local indebtedness was outstanding at that time. During the thirty years following 1790,
state and local governmental units of the new country, with the exception of
New York state, had only nominal debts or none at all. As late as 1825 the
aggregate debt of state governmental units was only $13 million and local
indebtedness was so low that no aggregate measure had been taken.[3]

The period from the late 1820's to 1837 was marked by rapid expansion
in all branches of economic activity. In an effort to attract trade and industry, the various governmental units, led by the states, vied with one another

[2]For example, assume that a municipal unit has $2 million of 5 per cent bonds
outstanding, a principal payment of $10 thousand due, and an overdue interest payment of
$50 thousand owed on $1 million of this indebtedness. Using the first definition, $2
million is the amount in default. Under the second definition, $1.05 million is the
amount in default. If the third definition is used, $60 thousand is the amount in default.

[3]The amount of state and local debt outstanding in 1825 and other selected years in
the 1800's appears in Table 6 (p. 34).

CHART 1
Defaults of State and Local Units, by Year Reported, 1839-1929

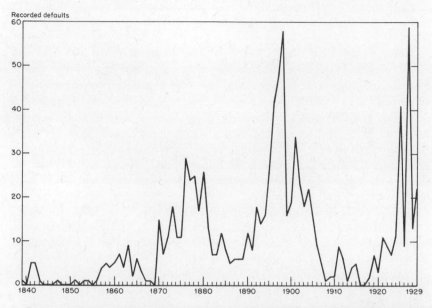

Sources: NBER compilations from issues of *The Bond Buyer;* Hillhouse, *Municipal Bonds;* Hillhouse, *Defaulted Municipal Bonds;* and Knappen, *Revenue Bonds.*

in the development of roads, canals, railroads and other public improvements. A period of feverish building and borrowing, especially in the mid-1830's, was the result. The panic of 1837 and the ensuing depression, which lasted well into the next decade, were accompanied by widespread defaults and losses, especially in state debt.

There were twelve defaults by state and local units reported as having started between 1839 and 1843. The number of units in default during this period seems small when compared with the number of units having newly reported defaults in most later periods (see Chart 1); however, the number of state and local units with debt outstanding was also very small.[4] Furthermore, the total indebtedness of the defaulting units was approximately $125 million, which was slightly over half of $245 million, the estimated average state and local debt outstanding in this period. The dollar amount of principal repudiated in this period totaled approximately $13.8 million and

---

[4]Thirty-seven state and local units were responsible for approximately $258 million of the estimated $260 million of debt outstanding in 1842. Lists of the individual units appear in *United States Magazine and Democratic Review*, XII (February, 1843), pp. 211-212 and U.S. Bureau of the Census, *Tenth Census of the United States: 1880. Valuation, Taxation, and Public Indebtedness*, VII, pp. 523-645.

approximately $1.3 million of interest due was never paid.[5]

There were only a few new defaults reported between 1843 and the start of the Civil War. Most of these defaults followed the recession of 1857 and were short in duration. The amount of final loss from these defaults was very small.

There were approximately thirty defaults during the Civil War. The real flood of defaults on state and local indebtedness started in 1870 and lasted through the early 1880's. The extent of these defaults became especially serious in the 1873 to 1879 depression period. The indebtedness of defaulting state and local units was approximately $245 million of the $1 billion average state and local indebtedness outstanding between 1873 and 1879. Many of the defaults in this period, especially those from the Southern region, can be classified as repudiations. The total loss of principal and interest due to defaults during the 1873-79 depression period was approximately $150 million.

A moderate number of new defaults occurred during the 1880's and early 1890's. However, the next time that defaults became a serious problem was the period following the Panic of 1893. Chart 1 shows that the number of recorded new defaults rose rapidly in the middle 1890's. The total indebtedness of state and local units which defaulted during the 1893-99 period, when the extent of defaults was the most serious, was $130 million, or approximately 10 per cent of the average total state and local indebtedness outstanding in that period. Approximately $25 million of principal and interest were lost because of the defaults during this period. While the number of units that reported new defaults stayed relatively large until 1906, most of the defaults in the early 1900's were small debt issues that were used to finance local real estate booms that subsequently collapsed or poorly managed irrigation projects in the Far West.

The number of state and local units with newly recorded defaults was relatively small from 1906 to the mid-1920's. Early indications of the state and local debt payment problems to come during the 1929 depression period appeared in three scattered areas. First, in Washington 55 local governmental units went into default on special assessment bonds between 1925 and 1927. Second, in 1927 the state of Arkansas was forced to assume approximately $53 million or one-third of the indebtedness incurred by Arkansas municipalities to prevent their possible default. Defaults by Florida municipalities also started in 1927, following the collapse of the Florida real estate boom in 1926.

From 1839 through 1929, every kind of governmental unit had recorded default situations. The number of units in default was rather evenly distribu-

[5]A detailed account of the amount of debt in default and the amount of final losses appears in Hempel, "Postwar Quality of Municipal Bonds," pp. 84-161.

ted among counties and parishes, incorporated municipalities, unincorporated municipalities and special districts. In dollar amounts, states accounted for more than half of the total amount defaulted over the entire period and incorporated municipalities led all other types of governmental units. Furthermore, the population figures for some 200 defaulting local governmental units, when compared with the total number of such units, show a much higher incidence of reported defaults in the more populous units.[6]

Payment Difficulties in the 1929 Depression Period

The depression beginning in 1929 was the most recent major default period. The record of state and local payment difficulties between 1929 and 1937 is examined in greater detail because more information is available for this period than any of the earlier ones. In late 1932, *The Daily Bond Buyer* began publishing information on the number of state and local units with indebtedness in default during the 1929 depression period. Chart 2 shows the monthly number of state and local units reported to have indebtedness in default by type of governmental unit from 1933-42. Because many defaults and recoveries from default were not reported to *The Daily Bond Buyer* until after they occurred, the figures in Chart 2 probably lag somewhat behind the actual situations. The figures in Chart 2 indicate that the total number of state and local units with indebtedness in default more than trebled from 1933-35 (the peak was 3,252 units in mid-1935) and then, by 1942, declined to approximately the early 1933 levels. One particularly noticeable characteristic revealed in Chart 2 is that slightly over one-third of the average total number of recorded defaults in 1935-37 were on special assessment or revenue bond issues.[7] A total of 4,771 state and local units was reported to have indebtedness in default sometime between 1929 and 1937.

The total indebtedness of state and local units with recorded defaults, 1929-37 was approximately $2.85 billion, which represented slightly over 15 per cent of the average amount of state and local debt outstanding in the early 1930's. The maximum total indebtedness of state and local units in default in a single year, approximately $2.8 billion, was reached in 1933, because nearly all defaults involving appreciable amounts of aggregate total debts were in effect by late 1933. This total began falling rapidly in 1934 and 1935 and had declined to approximately $0.2 billion (excluding repudiations)

---

[6]Detailed information on the number of defaults, the kinds of taxing districts involved and the geographic concentration of defaults for the 1839-1929 period may be found in Hempel, "Postwar Quality of Municipal Bonds," pp. 84-97 and in Table 4 (page 30 of this study).

[7]Special assessment and revenue bonds are described on pages 60 and 93-96.

CHART 2

Defaults of State and Local Units, by Month, 1933-42

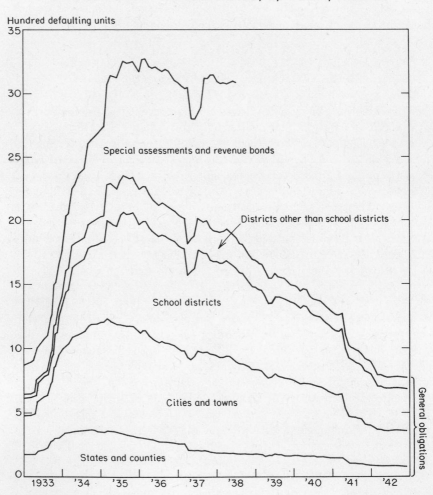

Hundred defaulting units

Special assessments and revenue bonds

Districts other than school districts

School districts

Cities and towns

States and counties

General obligations

1933   '34   '35   '36   '37   '38   '39   '40   '41   '42

Note: Special assessment default data is not available after May 1, 1938. State obligations include one default from January 1, 1933 to August 1, 1935 and two in April and May 1933.

Source: Default records of *The Daily Bond Buyer.*

by 1939.[8] The timing differences between the number of defaults and total indebtedness of units in default can be explained by the rapid and generally complete recoveries by most large governmental units which defaulted.

The dollar amount in default has been interpreted in two other ways. First, the overdue interest plus the debt upon which interest was in default from 1929-37 came to approximately $1,350 million, or 7.3 per cent of the average amount of state and local debt outstanding in the early 1930's.[9] Second, the past due interest and principal reached a maximum of approximately $320 million. This figure is slightly above 1.7 per cent of the average amount of state and local debt outstanding in the early 1930's; however, it is approximately 16 per cent of the estimated average annual charge for interest and redemption of principal.[10]

The extent and impact of defaults of state and local debts in the 1929 depression period can be assessed by looking at the composition of the aggregative figures. Table 1 evinces the number and total indebtedness of state and local units with recorded defaults from 1929 through 1937 by type of governmental unit. Its figures indicate that every type of political subdivision had default problems. Special districts other than school districts had the highest proportionate incidence of defaults, with reclamation, levee, irrigation and drainage districts leading the way. Towns and organized townships, states and school districts had the lowest proportionate incidence of defaults. The states were classified by the total number of units with recorded defaults from 1929-37. Five states had no default situations. Ten states had from one to ten default situations. Twelve states had from eleven to fifty default situations. Twelve states had from 50 to 200 default situations. Nine states had over 200 defaults.

Table 2 shows the indebtedness of the larger government units in default in fourteen states with serious statewide default problems. In eight of the nine states in which defaulting units numbered 200 or more, the default situation presented a serious statewide problem. In six other states, while the number of default situations was less than 200, conditions were serious enough to adversely affect the credit of these states and their local units. The indebtedness of the defaulting units with populations of over 5,000 in these fourteen states was $2.25 billion or approximately 79 per cent of the total indebtedness of all state and local units in default. In the remaining thirty-four states, there were either very few defaults or the problem appeared to be one of local areas or special districts rather than one of statewide importance.

One characteristic which differentiated the state and local debt payment

[8]Indebtedness figures are based on dollar amounts for units in default from *Moody's Municipal and Government Manual.*

[9]Chatters, *Municipal Debt Defaults,* p. 1.

[10]Estimated by the author using an average maturity of fifteen years and an average annual interest cost of 4.5 per cent.

TABLE 1

Incidence of Defaults by Type of Governmental Unit, 1929-37
(dollars are in millions)

Type of Governmental Unit	Total Number[a]	Number in Default[b]	Per Cent of Total Number in Default	Net Debt of All Units, 1932[c]	Indebtedness of Defaulting Unit[d]	Proportion of Debt in Default
States	48	1	2.1	$ 2,361	$ 160	6.8%
Counties	3,053	417	13.7	2,391	360	15.1
Incorporated municipalities	16,366	1,434	8.8	8,842	1,760	19.9
Towns and organized townships	20,262	88	.4	344	10	2.9
School districts	127,108	1,241	.9	2,040	160	7.8
Reclamation, levee, irrigation and drainage districts	3,351	944	28.2	1,599[e]	400[e]	25.0[e]
Other special districts	5,229	646	12.4			
Total	175,417	4,771	2.7	17,577	2,850	16.2

[a]Based on number in William Anderson, *The Units of Government in the United States*, Public Administration Service, Chicago, 1934, pp. 1 and 24.

[b]Based on all defaults reported to *The Daily Bond Buyer* from 1929 through 1937.

[c]U.S. Bureau of the Census, *Financial Statistics of State and Local Governments, 1932*, Washington, D.C., 1933.

[d]Indebtedness at time of default as reported in *The Daily Bond Buyer*.

[e]Combination of reclamation, levee, irrigation and drainage districts and other special districts.

TABLE 2

Amount of 1934 Indebtedness in Default by State and Local Units
With Population of Over 5,000, 1930 Census
(thousands of dollars)

Group 1[a]

Arkansas	346,142
Florida	299,863
Louisiana	90,616
Michigan	507,339
New Jersey	223,868
North Carolina	174,704
Ohio	273,471
Texas	151,865
Group 1 Total	2,067,868

Group 2

Alabama	35,477
Kentucky	13,842
Mississippi	27,929
Oklahoma	16,766
South Carolina	18,195
Tennessee	67,538
Group 2 Total	179,747
Total for Both Groups	2,247,615

Source: Data from *The Daily Bond Buyer.*

[a]Defaulting governmental units in state numbered 200 or more.

difficulties in the 1929 depression period from similar experiences in previous major default periods was the high incidence of repayment of defaulted principal and interest in a comparatively short period. Nearly all of the large state and local units in default made complete payment of all due debt service charges within a few years. For example, all of the forty-eight cities with populations over 25,000 that were in default in this depression period were reported out of default by 1938. Among these defaulting cities, five solved their defaults without any change of contract, twenty-eight did not scale interest or principal in their refunding operation, fifteen scaled interest only in their refunding operation and no city in this group had any reduction of principal. In 1939, with the state default cured and nearly all of the defaults in larger municipal units corrected, the accumulated past due interest and principal (after repudiations were eliminated) did not exceed $50 million for state and local units with populations over 10,000. By 1946 nearly all of the units with populations over 10,000 that had not repudiated their debts had settled their default problems.

The payment records for smaller municipal units which were recorded as defaulting in the 1929 depression period are less complete and less impressive than the payment records of the larger units which defaulted in the same period. The only available information on the majority of these smaller defaulting municipal units is found in the records of the cases filed under the Federal Municipal Bankruptcy Act of 1937.[11] The primary aim of this Act was to force recalcitrant creditors into line when a satisfactory and equitable agreement between the municipal unit and its creditors had been reached.

Table 3 summarizes the results of the cases filed by municipal units under the Federal Municipal Bankruptcy Act of 1937 from fiscal 1938 through fiscal 1966. Nearly all of the 353 municipal units that filed petitions under this Act had populations of less than 10,000. Over half of the petitions which were filed were for special districts. Admitted losses were slightly over one-third of the admitted debts in default and approximately $70 million of the losses were on municipal bonds that defaulted in the 1929 depression period.[12]

The total loss of principal and interest resulting from recorded defaults during the 1929 depression period is estimated at $100 million, or about .5 per cent of the average amount of state and local debt outstanding in the period. Nearly 70 per cent of these losses were settled under the Federal Municipal Bankruptcy Act.[13] The loss figures do not include lower interest payments on refunding issues or accured interest on unpaid principal or interest.

The payment difficulties of revenue bonds are also noteworthy because

---

[11] An earlier Municipal Bankruptcy Act with a similar purpose was enacted in 1934, but was declared unconstitutional in 1936. There were eighty-nine petitions filed under the 1934 Act before it was declared unconstitutional.

[12] Henry W. Lehman, "The Federal Municipal Bankruptcy Act," *Journal of Finance*, V, No. 3, September 1960, pp. 241-256.

[13] Minority creditors did not have the same temptation to fight in default situations where (1) principal and interest were paid within a few years, or (2) the only relief requested by the municipal unit was an extension of maturity dates, or a slight lowering of the interest rate for a few years, as they did in situations where (3) the municipal unit desired to scale down principal or interest or both substantially. Most of the default situations in the 1929 depression period were settled by the first two methods.

TABLE 3

Summary of the Results of Cases Filed Under the Federal Municipal Bankruptcy Act of 1937

Fiscal Year	Cases Filed	Cases Concluded	Cases Dismissed	Admitted Debts	Statistics for Cases Concluded	
					Amount Paid or to be Paid as Extended	Admitted Losses
1938	35	2	0	$ 67,675	$ 67,675	$ 0
1939	71	17	0	6,587,012	3,924,149	2,662,863
1940	104	22	7	15,500,000	6,674,000	8,826,000
1941	19	37	8	28,466,000	16,332,000	12,134,000
1942	43	46	3	33,704,000	24,458,000	9,246,000
1943	13	40	23	26,633,000	16,032,000	10,601,000
1944	5	18	2	18,014,000	11,457,000	6,557,000
1945	8	14	3	39,816,000	27,185,000	12,631,000
1946	7	8	1	13,086,555	9,594,984	3,491,571
1947	7	8	4	4,651,168	2,715,234	1,935,934
1948	7	12	1	2,464,215	1,632,987	831,228
1949	2	2	0	224,361	136,525	87,836
1950	4	5	5	1,253,183	464,094	789,089
1951	3	3	1	1,308,687	582,868	725,819
1952	15	17	1	10,043,648	8,424,662	1,618,986
1953	0	2	2	2,183,413	1,163,615	1,019,798
1954	2	4	23	934,733	353,562	581,171
1955	1	0	0	—	—	—
1956	1	1	1	639,095	211,300	427,795
1957	0	2	0	2,171,448	1,629,448	542,000
1958	2	1	0	16,124	16,124	0
1959	3	3	0	2,077,382	544,668	1,532,714
1960	0	1	0	106,500	106,500	0
1961	0	0	0	—	—	—
1962	1	3	1	972,642	544,668	427,974
1963	0	0	0	—	—	—
1964	0	0	0	—	—	—
1965	0	0	0	—	—	—
1966	0	0	0	—	—	—
Total	353	268	85	210,920,841	134,251,063	76,669,778

Source: Administrative Office of the United States Courts.

the 1929-37 period is the first major default period in which state and local indebtedness payable solely from specified revenues was outstanding. The first revenue bonds issued by a state or local unit in this country were offered by Spokane, Washington, in the 1890's. The number and dollar amount of revenue bonds issued grew slowly. By 1925 revenue bonds constituted approximately one-half of 1 per cent of total dollar amount of state and local debt outstanding. The proportionate dollar share of indebtedness accounted for by revenue bonds rose to approximately 2 per cent in 1931, approximately 3½ per cent in 1934 and approximately 5 per cent in 1937.[14]

There were only twelve instances of state and local revenue bond defaults recorded from 1929 through 1937.[15] The dollar value of these twelve defaulting revenue issues was approximately $18.7 million, which is 5.8 per cent of the approximately $325 million of revenue bonds outstanding in 1931, 3.1 per cent of the approximately $600 million of revenue bonds outstanding in 1934 and 1.9 per cent of the approximately $1 billion of revenue bonds oustanding in 1937. These percentage figures are below the proportionate dollar amount of all state and local indebtedness involved in default situations; however, losses of principal and interest on defaulting revenue bonds were proportionately much higher than similar losses on all defaulting state and local indebtedness. The total amount of principal repudiated or scaled down was approximately $6.6 million, which is over one-third of the total revenue bond principal in default.[16]

Payment Difficulties in the Postwar Period

Difficulties with state and local debt service payments have been relatively limited during the long period of prosperity following World War II. Information on payment difficulties in the postwar period was obtained from intensive searches through postwar indexes and issues of *The Daily Bond Buyer, Moody's Municipal and Governments Manual, The Wall Street Journal,* and *The Commercial and Financial Chronicle;* examinations of *The Daily Bond Buyer's* default records and its correspondence in connection with its default survey in 1959; correspondence with the Administrative Office of the United States Courts and with various state and local officials; and interviews with

[14]The aggregate dollar amount of state and local revenue bonds issued annually is presented in Appendix Table 1. Detailed descriptions of early issues and aggregate dollar amount outstanding figures can be found in John F. Fowler, *Revenue Bonds,* New York, 1938; and Laurence S. Knappen, *Revenue Bonds and the Investor,* New York, 1939.

[15]The only recorded default on a state and local revenue bond prior to 1929 was on the $300 thousand water revenue bonds of the city of Centralia, Washington, in 1919. This default was primarily technical and both principal and interest were eventually fully paid.

[16]See Hempel, "Postwar Quality of Municipal Bonds," pp. 119-122 for a detailed description of each of these twelve revenue bond default situations.

and information from several regulatory commissions and the major municipal bond rating agencies.[17]

The combined information from all of the preceding sources reveals 329 reported state and local debt default situations from 1945-65. Despite the wide variety of sources, the information on many of these default situations is limited and incomplete. This is because there is no central agency recording default information and because publicity is often disadvantageous to both the debtor unit and the limited number of its creditors. It seems incorrect to make direct comparisons of the total number of debt payment difficulties in this period with the total number of debt payment difficulties in previous periods because listings of defaulted securities on bank examinations were not available in previous periods. Many of the 266 postwar state and local default situations which were reported only on bank examinations may have been temporary or technical. Most of these 266 situations involved smaller municipal units and small quantities and nearly all were locally held — 181, or 68 per cent, were found to be held by banks in the same city, town or county and 77, or 29 per cent, more were held by banks within the same state.

A few characteristics of the total number of defaulted situations are discernible. Of the 329 reported default situations, 115, or 35 per cent, were on short-term state and local debts, 92, or 27 per cent, were by special districts other than school districts and 47, or 14.3 per cent, were on revenue bonds. The time distribution of the default situation for which the date of default was available revealed that there was at least one default in every year studied after World War II, no noticeable cyclical pattern in recorded defaults due to the relatively mild postwar recessions, and an increasing trend in the absolute number of reported defaults in the postwar period.

The dollar amount of state and local debt in default provides a clearer answer about the extent of the debt payment difficulties in the postwar period. The principal actually in default and the principal upon which interest is in default at the time of the difficulty totals approximately $325 million for all state and local units which have defaulted from 1945-65. This total is slightly over .3 per cent of the total state and local debt outstanding at the end of the 1965 fiscal year. Approximately $294 million, or 91 per cent, of the estimated total amount of principal in default is the responsibility of twenty-seven municipal units involved in major default situations.[18] All but six of these major default situations were on revenue bonds.

[17]These commissions and agencies are The Federal Deposit Insurance Corporation, The Board of Governors of the Federal Reserve Bank, the Committee for the Valuation of Securities for Life Insurance Commissioners, Standard and Poor's Corporation, Moody's Investors Service, Inc., and Dun and Bradstreet.

[18]The term major default situation is used to describe well-documented default situations that are clearly neither temporary nor technical and that involve at least $200 thousand of principal in default or principal upon which interest is in default.

Chart 3 shows the dollar amount of principal in default or principal upon which interest is in default and interest payments in default for the twenty-seven major default situations from 1948, the year of the first major postwar default, through 1965. This chart is clearly dominated by the $133 million West Virginia Turnpike default in 1958 and the $101 million Calumet Skyway default in 1963. Principal in default or upon which interest is in default totaled approximately $278 million; interest in default (excluding interest on unpaid interest), approximately $32 million in 1965. The amount of permanent losses of principal and interest from state and local defaults starting in

CHART 3
Dollar Amount of Principal and Interest in Default, 1948-65

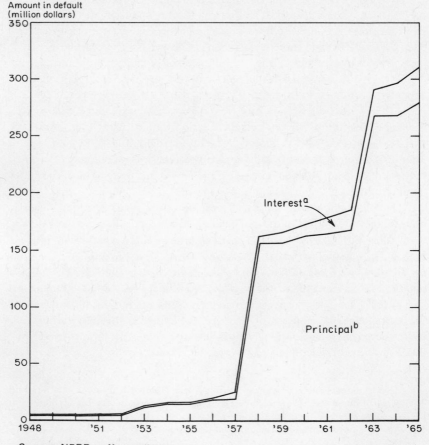

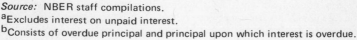

Source: NBER staff compilations.

[a]Excludes interest on unpaid interest.

[b]Consists of overdue principal and principal upon which interest is overdue.

the postwar period totaled $8-9 million, with most of these losses settled under the Municipal Bankruptcy Act (see Table 3, page 25).

Summary

Two general conclusions may be made about the time distribution of the recorded defaults and losses on state and local debt from the first default in 1839 through 1965. The first is that defaults occurred, nearly continuously, after the amount of indebtedness became significant, under both good and bad economic conditions. The rather common belief that defaults occur only in depression periods is obviously false. Second, it was only in major depression periods that the extent of defaults on state and local indebtedness spread to dangerous proportions or that the volume of losses rose to a level that affected the over-all economy.

The recorded defaults from 1839 through 1965 shown in Table 4 support the first general conclusion. The data in Table 4 also show that defaults occurred in every major type of governmental unit and in every geographical region. In addition, Table 4 demonstrates that the number of recorded defaults grew rapidly during and immediately following the four depression periods which can be classified as major default and loss periods for state and local indebtedness — 1837-43, 1873-79, 1893-99 and 1929-37.

Table 5 shows the dollar amount of defaults and losses on state and local bonds in each of these major default periods. The total indebtedness of defaulting state and local units was the highest proportion of state and local debt outstanding in the 1837-43 period. This proportion did not always decline in later periods, however, because the total indebtedness of defaulting state and local units was proportionately greater in the 1929-37 period than in the 1893-99 period. Figures for the two alternative methods of measuring the amount of state and local debt which has been in default — the overdue interest plus the amount of debt upon which interest is in default and the past due interest and principal — are available only for the 1929-37 period. The data in Table 5 also indicate that the proportionate amount of permanent losses of principal and interest was highest during the 1873-79 period, when there were numerous repudiations, and lowest in the 1929-37 period.

TABLE 4

Recorded Defaults from 1839 Through 1965, by Type of Governmental Unit and Geographical Region

	1839 -49	1850 -59	1860 -69	1870 -79	1880 -89	1890 -99	1900 -09	1910 -19	1920 -29	1930 -39	1940 -49	1950 -59	1960 -65	Total Defaults	State and Local Governmental Unit in 1962[a]
By Type of Unit:															
States	9	2	1	9					1					22	50
Counties and parishes		7	15	57	30	94	43	7	15	417	6	12	17	720	3,043
Incorp. munics.	4	4	13	50	30	93	51	17	39	1,434	31	31	70	1,867	17,997
Unincorp. munics.		4	9	46	31	50	33	5	10	88	7	4	20	307	17,144
School districts				4	5	9	11		14	1,241	5	23	41	1,353	34,678
Other districts				2	1	12	11	7	107	1,590	30	42	44	1,846	18,323
By Geographical Region:															
New England states[b]	1		1	1	1	2	13	1	1	7			4	19	2,719
Middle Atlantic states[c]	2	5	6	19	11	13	13	4	4	251	9	4	10	351	11,963
Southern states[d]	6		2	40	29	36	25	9	51	1,864	16	33	56	2,167	8,859
Midwestern states[e]	4	10	28	84	46	89	68	6	18	1,152	18	34	73	1,630	44,649
Southwestern states[f]			1	20	7	79	27	5	25	706	25	36	35	966	11,384
Mountain states[g]				2		17	2	8	17	270	6	4	3	329	4,443
Pacific states[h]		2		2	3	22	14	3	70	520	5	1	11	653	7,218
Totals	13	17	38	168	97	258	149	36	186	4,770	79	112	192	6,115	91,235

Notes to Table 4

Sources: Default information in *The Daily Bond Buyer, The Commercial and Financial Chronicle,* and *The Investment Banker's Association Bulletin;* default lists from Federal Deposit Insurance Corporation, Life Insurance Commission, and U.S. Courts; Albert M. Hillhouse, *Defaulted Municipal Bonds,* Municipal Financial Officers Association, Chicago, 1935; and B.W. Ratchford, *American State Debts,* Durham, N.C., 1941. Number of governmental units based on data from Government Division of U.S. Bureau of the Census.

[a]The number of governmental units has changed rapidly. For example, in 1932 there were 127,108 school districts, 8,580 other districts, and 175,369 state and local governmental units.

[b]Connecticut, Maine, Massachusetts, New Hampshire, Rhode Island and Vermont.

[c]Delaware, District of Columbia, Maryland, New Jersey, New York and Pennsylvania.

[d]Alabama, Arkansas, Florida, Georgia, Kentucky, Louisiana, Mississippi, North Carolina, South Carolina, Tennessee, Virginia and West Virginia.

[e]Illinois, Indiana, Iowa, Michigan, Minnesota, Missouri, Nebraska, Ohio, North Dakota and Wisconsin.

[f]Arizona, Kansas, New Mexico, Oklahoma and Texas.

[g]Colorado, Idaho, Montana, Nevada, Utah and Wyoming.

[h]Alaska, California, Hawaii, Oregon and Washington.

TABLE 5

Comparison of the Extent of Defaults by State and Local Units in Major Default Periods
(dollar figures in thousands)

Period	Average State and Local Debt Outstanding	Total Indebtedness of Defaulting State and Local Units	Per Cent of Debt Outstanding	Past Due Interest and Principal[a]	Per Cent of Debt Outstanding	Loss of Principal and Interest[b]	Per Cent of Debt Outstanding
1837-43	$ 245,000	$ 125,000	51.0	n.a.	–	$ 15,000	6.1
1873-79	1,000,000	245,000	24.5	n.a.	–	150,000	15.0
1893-99	1,300,000	130,000	10.0	n.a.	–	25,000	1.9
1929-37	18,500,000	2,850,000[c]	15.4	320,000[c]	1.7	100,000	.5

Source: Based on data from George H. Hempel, "The Postwar Quality of Municipal Bonds" unpublished dissertation, University of Michigan, 1964, pp. 84-161.

[a]Does not include interest on unpaid interest.

[b]Does not include interest on unpaid interest, interest due after a debt was repudiated or interest lost due to refunding at a lower interest cost.

[c]Overdue interest plus debt upon which interest is in default was $1,355,000 or 7.3 per cent of debt outstanding in 1929-37. This figure is not available for the earlier default periods.

n.a. = not available.

4

IDENTIFICATION OF
CHARACTERISTICS DENOTING QUALITY

In this chapter the historical record of instrument and borrower characteristics as indicators of state and local debt difficulties is examined. The borrower and instrument characteristics that were indicators of past payment problems are examined in two ways: first, identifying the aggregate characteristics that seem to have led to the heavy incidence of defaults and losses in each of the four major default periods; second, classifying the historically significant characteristics according to the primary groupings of variables for the conceptual model developed in Chater 2. Cross sections of available instrument and borrower characteristics for defaulting and nondefaulting issues are analyzed.

Characteristics Corresponding with Past Payment Difficulties

The first major default and loss period was in 1839-43. Some of the primary characteristics leading to the heavy incidence of defaults and losses are apparent, despite the scarcity of data. Table 6 shows that net state and local debt increased from $13 million in 1825 to $51 million in 1835, $196 million in 1840 and $260 million in 1843. Table 6 also shows that between 85 and 90 per cent of this indebtedness was incurred by states, most of this debt for purposes of indicating questionable financial prudence. Census data reveals that 95 per cent of the state indebtedness outstanding in 1838 was for private or state enterprises such as banking, canals, railroads and turnpikes.[1]

It is doubtful that any measure of wealth or income indicating potential cash inflows increased as rapidly as the state and local debt service charges that resulted from the increased indebtedness. A large proportion of state

---

[1]The *Tenth Census,* VII, p. 526 showed gross state indebtedness of $54 million for banking, $60 million for canals, $43 million for railroads, $7 million for turnpikes and $8 million for other purposes.

TABLE 6

Estimated Net State and Local Debt Outstanding in Selected
Periods, 1825-1902
(in millions of dollars)

| Year | Net State and Local Debt[a] | | Net State Debt | Net Local Debt |
	Total	Per Capita		
1825	13	1	13^b	n^c
1835	51	3	46^b	5^c
1840	196	12	176^d	20^e
1843	260	14	232^f	28^b
1850	230	10	190^e	40^c
1860	457	15	257^g	200^e
1870	869	23	353^g	516^g
1880	1,096	22	275^h	821^h
1890	1,137	18	211^h	926^h
1902	1,869	24	239^h	$1,630^h$

[a]Net state and local debt computed by adding net state debt and net local debt. Per capita debt computed using Bureau of the Census population figures.

[b]R.E. Badger and H.G. Guthmann, *Investment Principles and Practices*, New York, 1951, pp. 555-558.

[c]Estimated from indebtedness of large cities described in Hillhouse, *Municipal Bonds*, pp. 31-34; William L. Raymond, *State and Municipal Bonds*, Boston, 1932, pp. 295-298; and H.C. Adams, *Public Debts*, New York, 1890, pp. 341-344.

[d]Estimated from Census figures of $164 million in 1839 and $190 million in 1841 in U.S. Bureau of the Census, *Tenth Census of the United States: 1880. Valuation, Taxation, and Public Indebtedness*, VII, p. 281.

[e]Paul Strudenski, *Public Borrowing*, National Municipal League, New York, 1930, pp. 5-13.

[f]*U.S. Magazine and Democratic Review*, XII, (February 1843), pp. 211-212. These figures are probably gross debt; however, debt offsets were probably small at that time.

[g]U.S. Bureau of the Census, *Tenth Census*, VII, pp. 281-285.

[h]U.S. Department of Commerce, *Wealth, Debt, and Taxation, 1913*, I, pp. 38, 234-235.

n = negligible or amount probably less than $.5 million.

revenues in the 1830's probably came from debt-financed private or state enterprises. The severe depression following the Panic of 1837 led to a large decline in the wealth and income of most state and local units. Many of the revenue-producing enterprises either failed completely or ran at a loss. Additional debt financing temporarily kept some states from defaulting but also increased the amount of service charges, which had to be paid from declining cash inflows. As the incidence of defaults increased, this temporary source of cash was cut off. States committed nine of the twelve defaults and accounted for the entire amount of permanent losses in this period.[2]

Unwillingness to pay was also an important factor in this default period. Once debt-financed private or state banks, canals, railroads and turnpikes proved unsuccessful, state officials and residents seem to have felt that the bondholders rather than the borrowers should bear the brunt of the loss.

Many of the instrument and borrower characteristics that led to the first major default and loss period recurred as casual factors in the second major default and loss period, 1873-79. After declining from the early 1840's to the early 1850's, state and local debt began to rise rapidly. Table 6 shows that aggregate net state and local debt nearly doubled from 1850 to 1860 and from 1860 to 1870. The indebtedness of units in the South (excluding the debts of Confederate states which were declared invalid at the end of the Civil War) grew more rapidly than total state and local indebtedness. The majority of Southern borrowing was spent on waterworks, railroad facilities, Civil War expenditures and reconstruction.[3]

The rapidly rising cost of servicing the increased indebtedness did not appear to be matched by a commensurate increase in wealth or income measures indicating potential cash inflows. The estimated true value of real and personal property declined approximately 18 per cent in the Southern states from 1860 to 1870.[4] A serious downturn starting in 1873 reduced wealth and income in all sections of the country. As the depression dragged on, a rising number of poorly conceived railroad ventures failed or became financially dependent. The combination of heavy fixed costs, sometimes contracted for questionable purposes, and declining cash inflows proved too great a burden in many cases.

Financial prudence and willingness to pay was questionable in many of the resulting defaults and losses. Public funds were frequently used for private interests financing railroads. The optimistic predictions regarding the earning

---

[2]More detail and supporting evidence for the defaults in this period appears in Ratchford, *American State Debts*, pp. 1-161.

[3]*Tenth Census*, VII, pp. 283-293.

[4]*Ibid.*, VII, pp. 7-8.

TABLE 7

Recorded Defaults from 1839 Through 1929, by Primary Purpose of Indebtedness

By Purpose of Debt:	1839-44	1845-54	1855-59	1860-64	1865-69	1870-74	1875-79	1880-84	1885-89	1890-94	1895-99	1900-04	1905-09	1910-14	1915-19	1920-24	1925-29	Totals
General[a]	1	3			1	9	13	7	3	6	36	23	7	3	1	12	17	142
Education						1	5	4	4	4	11	13	1	3	1	2	18	67
Governmental bldgs.				2		4	2	2	3	4	16	8	1		1		2	45
Water and sewer	1		1				1	1	2	3	7	10	4	3	3	2	3	40
Other utilities							1				3	2				1	2	9
Roads and bridges					4	1	5			4	14	6	3	2	4	11	11	65
Flood control						2	1	1		2	10	10	3	5	2	7	22	65
Banking and canals	8																	8
Railroads	2	1	13	25	6	41	70	41	17	33	49	28	5	2	1			334
Other pvt. enterprises						3	5	5	1	2	10	3	1					30
Special assessments							1	1				3	1	2	1	1	12	22
Local improvements																4	55	59
Funding and refunding						1	3	4	1	10	34	9	8	2		2	2	76
Total defaults	12	4	14	27	11	62	106	66	31	68	190	115	34	22	14	42	144	962

Note: Excludes bonds of governmental unit before they became part of the United States and repudiations of Civil War debts of Confederate states acquired when they were not part of the United States.

Sources: Default information in *The Daily Bond Buyer, The Commercial and Financial Chronicle,* and *The Investment Banker's Association Bulletin;* Albert M. Hillhouse, *Defaulted Municipal Bonds,* Municipal Financial Officers Association, Chicago, 1935; B.W. Ratchford, *American State Debts,* Durham, N.C., 1941; and William L. Raymond, *State and Municipal Bonds,* Boston, 1932.

[a]Many of these issues were connected with Civil War and post-Civil War expenditures in the 1870's and 1880's. After that time the majority of these issues were used to finance the development of the issuing area.

power of the sponsored projects often failed to materialize, leaving the governmental unit and its taxpayers saddled with a heavy debt. Table 7 shows that approximately two-thirds of the defaults in this period were on debts issued to finance railroad facilities. The largest dollar amount in default and the majority of the permanent losses were by Southern state and local units. After the Civil War, many of the Southern governmental units were overrun by dishonest politicians who engaged in speculative activities and sometimes carried away the proceeds of debts incurred in the name of the governing body. In addition, some short-sighted Southern governmental units took advantage of the politically popular opportunity to repudiate debts which had been used in their interest.[5]

After declining slightly in the late 1870's aggregate state and local debt grew rapidly through the mid-1890's. Table 6 shows that all of this growth was due to increased local indebtedness. The outstanding indebtedness of states declined in this period. By 1890, net state debt was slightly less than 20 per cent of net state and local debt, lower than net state debt had been in the 1840's. Real estate booms in the central and western sectors of the United States were a major cause in the growth of local indebtedness. General improvements, railroads, roads, bridges, water facilities, etc., in these fast growing areas were financed by local issues.[6]

Defaults and losses on state and local debts became a serious economic problem again after the panic and depression of 1893 lowered wealth and income, sources of potential cash inflows. None of the defaults in this period were by state governments. Aggregate state debt service charges had fallen since the mid-1870's.[7] Many of the local defaults were caused by the collapse of speculative real estate booms, which had been aided by local borrowing. When the planned increases in local cash inflows failed to materialize, many units were unable to pay their high debt service costs. Table 4 shows that the number of defaults was highest in the central and western regions of the United States. The primary purposes for which the defaulting local debts had been issued were railroads, general improvements and funding and refunding, as Table 7 shows.

Once again, unwillingness to pay and the lack of financial prudence contributed to local defaults and losses. Private interests, such as real estate speculators and railroads, had encouraged borrowing beyond the unit's existing capacity to pay. Many officials and taxpayers in the local units were willing to borrow to encourage growth, but unwilling to pay the subsequently increased taxes when this growth failed to materialize.

---

[5]The causes of and amounts involved in many of these Southern default situations are described in Ratchford, *American State Debts,* pp. 162-229 and Hillhouse, *Municipal Bonds,* pp. 39-61.

[6]Hillhouse, *Municipal Bonds,* pp. 39-44.

[7]Ratchford, *American State Debts,* pp. 253-258.

There is more information about the aggregate characteristics leading to the fourth, and most recent, major default and loss period. State and local debt grew rapidly in the early 1900's. State and local debt outstanding grew from $4.4 billion in 1913 to $19 billion in 1931. The growth in this form of debt became particularly rapid after the end of World War I through 1931 when debt limits were hurdled, new overlapping governmental units were created, old state and local services were expanded and many new ones were added. The yearly amount of long-term state and local debt issued had never exceeded $500 million before 1919. In every year from 1921 through 1931 the yearly amount exceeded $1.1 billion and the annual average for that period was nearly $1.4 billion.[8]

State and local cash inflows did not increase nearly as rapidly as did the debt service charges. Wealth and income, grew at a slower pace than state and local debt. From 1919 through 1928 the coverage of net state and local debt by net wealth fell from 71.1 times to 35.0 times and the ratio of net state and local debt to national income increased from .076 to .156.[9]

The depression starting in 1929 severely lowered both wealth and income. In 1932 the coverage of net state and local debt by net wealth had fallen to 19.5 times and the ratio of net state and local debt to national income increased to .388. Figures for the coverage of interest and estimated debt service charges by state and local revenues are available for 1922 and 1932. Interest payments were 8.3 per cent and estimated debt service charges were 12.7 per cent of state and local revenues in 1922. In 1932 interest payments had risen to 10.7 per cent and estimated debt service charges to 19.7 per cent of state and local revenues.[10]

It is possible to investigate other aspects of the cash inflows available to meet the rapidly rising debt service charges during this period. Total state and local revenues remained at approximately the same level from 1927 through 1934, but the sources of these revenues shifted considerably. Cash revenues from property taxes declined approximately $700 million, from 60 per cent to 48 per cent of total revenues during the period, primarily because assessed

[8]See Appendix Tables 1 and 2 for yearly figures.

[9]See Appendix Table 4 for yearly figures.

[10]U. S. Bureau of the Census, *Historical Statistics on State and Local Government Finances, 1902-1953,* Special Studies Number 38, 1955, pp. 17-18. Principal due was estimated by taking the difference between long-term debt issued and net change in long-term debt for the year. This figure is conservative because some debt was issued to replace outstanding debt.

[11]Chart 16 (p. 74) shows that the proportion of property taxes that were uncollected in cities with over 50 thousand residents rose from 4.7 per cent in 1928 to 26.3 per cent in 1933.

property values declined and the proportion of property taxes that were not collected rose.[11] On the other hand, state and local revenues from the federal government increased approximately $900 million, from 1 per cent of the total state and local revenues in 1927 to 12 per cent in 1934. Despite employee cutbacks, payless paydays and large reductions in capital outlays, state and local cash outflows excluding debt service charges proved very difficult to cut. Current operating expenditures were higher in the early 1930's than they were in 1927, and assistance and subsidies increased from $93 million in 1927 to $815 million in 1934.[12]

At first the effects of high debt service costs, unexpanding revenues and rising expenditure requirements were overcome by skipping sinking fund payments, by reducing liquid assets and by additional borrowing. Short-term debt secured by anticipated or uncollected property taxes was a popular source of cash, but added to the burgeoning debt service costs. When the financial pressures persisted[13] and the temporary sources of cash dried up because of bank failures, high interest costs and loss of public confidence in state and local debts, many governmental units were forced to default. The number of defaults in this period would have been much greater if many state and local units had not forced funding and refunding issues on bondholders and had not used the proceeds from federally aided relief debt issues to meet debt service payments.

Financial prudence and willingness to pay would be questioned in some of the default situations in the 1929-37 period. Some state and local units were forced to default because of the lack of financial planning and the generally poor quality of many governmental administrations. Special assessment or local improvement districts were created to permit the improvement of undeveloped and speculative areas. Some debts which were issued depended entirely on the future growth of wealth and income in the area. In some cases, the officers of real estate companies became officials of local units and promoted bond issues to develop their companies' properties. Finally, a few small communities appear to have decided that bondholders should bear part of their costs. Nevertheless, the incidence of excessive financial mismanagement or widespread unwillingness to pay in this default period was relatively less than the incidence in any of the previous major default periods. This contention is supported by the relatively rapid and complete recovery in most of the larger default situations and the small amount of permanent losses

[12]State and local revenues and expenditures for selected years from 1922 through 1968 appear in Tables 10 (p. 56) and 11 (p.63), respectively.

[13]For example, Census data indicates that in 1932 total state and local revenues were $7,887 million, state and local expenditures (excluding all debt service charges) $7,563 million, interest expenses $840 million and estimated long-term principal payments due probably was approximately $1,400 million.

relative to the amount of debt in default.

The analysis of the time distribution of defaults in the preceding chapter indicated that defaults occurred almost continuously. Several instrument and borrower characteristics recurred frequently as indicators of the default situations in times other than the major default and loss periods.[14] First, some defaulting governmental units contracted for debt service charges that were clearly above the minimum cash flows they could reasonably anticipate. Second, some defaulting units suffered severe declines in cash revenues due to natural catastrophes or economic declines in the area or industry on which the unit was dependent. It would have been difficult to have predicted some of these declines; however, many of the units which were forced to default had allowed themselves very little margin for such contingencies. Third, Table 8 (p.44) demonstrates that many of the bonds which defaulted in times other than the major default periods were issued to finance railroad facilities and other private ventures. If these enterprises failed, many state and local units were either unable or unwilling to pay the debt service charges contracted in financing the enterprises. Finally, poor financial planning and dishonest or inept officials led to some default situations.

Aggregate Historical Characteristics Conforming
with the Conceptual Model

The instrument and borrower characteristics that were significant in the past seem to conform closely with the conceptual model formulated in Chapter 2. The defaults on state and local debts were caused by the issuing unit having inadequate cash flows available to meet debt service charges or by unwillingness to pay on the part of the issuing unit. In the past, defaults and losses on state and local debt became a serious problem only when economic declines lowered wealth and income to the point that it significantly affected cash inflows. Prior to each of the major default periods, however, certain instrument and borrower characteristics indicated that state and local units were vulnerable to economic declines. Most of these same characteristics were also indicators of defaults in periods other than depressions. The objective of the following paragraphs is to identify the aggregate characteristics that indicated vulnerability in the past.

The debt service charges which must be paid are the first variable in the conceptual model. A rapid increase in the amount of debt outstanding, a surrogate for debt service charges, occurred before each of the four major

---

[14]The characteristics for individual issues rather than aggregate characteristics had to be considered for the default situations in times other than the major default and loss periods.

default periods and prior to many individual default situations. Debt service charge figures are often available for individual units; however, there are no aggregate debt service charge figures available at the present time. The amount of debt outstanding should be adjusted for changes in interest costs and in the retirement schedule or sinking fund requirements when such figures are available.

The expected over-all cash inflows during the period of the indebtedness are the second variable. Current state and local revenues by themselves are an inadequate measure. Expected over-all cash inflows also depend on wealth and income levels, acceptable rates of taxation or payment for services, and potential short-term sources of cash. Wealth and income measures, which are indicative of potential cash inflows, seem to have risen less rapidly than estimated debt service charges before each of the four major default periods. These measures then declined absolutely in the economic decline immediately preceding the heavy incidence of defaults. The aggregate wealth and income measures observed included population, total net wealth, assessed property value, estimated full property value, national income and disposable personal income.

There is no quantitative information about the amount of taxes or payments for services that people are willing to pay. However, state and local units were generally unable to raise tax rates in periods when income and wealth were declining. Temporary sources of cash inflows appear to have been used to prevent defaults immediately prior to the major default periods. In each major default period, state and local indebtedness increased very rapidly in the two or three years between the start of an economic decline and the period when the incidence of defaults and losses became heavy. State and local units reduced their cash and security holding slightly over 15 per cent from 1929 to 1933. The majority of the remaining assets were state and local securities.[15] Figures for state and local cash and security holdings are not available for the other major default periods.

The relationships between debt service charges and the wealth measures indicating potential cash inflows give only a partial picture of prospective quality. The expected cash expenditures or outflows that have priority over debt service charges, the third variable in the conceptual model, must also be considered. Whether or not a governmental unit is able to meet its debt service charges is determined by the minimum difference between cash inflows and cash outflows that are paid before debt service charges. In the past this minimum difference has always occurred when cash revenues had declined. For this reason, the level of expenditures as cash revenues decline is

[15]Raymond W. Goldsmith, Robert E. Lipsey and Morris Mendelson, *Studies in the National Balance Sheet of the United States,* Vol. II, Princeton for NBER, 1963, Table III-6a, pp. 218-219.

emphasized. In the past, some expenditures requiring cash outlays have risen, some have stayed relatively constant, and some declined when cash inflows have declined.

Aggregate state and local expenditures were classified by character and function for several years prior to and during the 1929 default period. Despite austerity programs by many individual units, state and local units were unable to reduce aggregate current outlays in this period. The expenditures for current outlays were slightly higher in 1932 and 1934 than they had been in 1927. By 1934 state and local capital outlays had declined approximately 40 per cent from their 1927 level. The entire decline was absorbed by the increase in expenditures for assistance and subsidies. Classified according to function, expenditures for education, highways, sanitation and recreation fell significantly from 1927 to 1934. But expenditures for such functions as hospitals, health, police and fire protection and general control remained about the same; and those for public welfare and natural resources increased significantly from 1927 to 1934.[16]

The borrower's financial prudence and willingness to pay is the fourth variable in the conceptual model. The influence is strictly negative, as financial prudence and willingness to pay cannot create additional wealth or income for the borrower. Financial prudence and willingness to pay are often assumed for all state and local governmental units; however, inadequacies in these basic traits have recurred as causal factors in all four of the major default periods. Unwillingness to pay has led to the majority of the permanent losses in these periods. These characteristics also show up as a major cause of defaults in less extreme periods.

Poor financial planning and management, a lack of financial prudence, existed in many state and local units prior to the actual default as well as in many nondefaulting units. However, many of the units which defaulted would not have done so had they adequate financial planning and management. Very few instrument and borrower characteristics are available to measure the financial prudence of the borrower. Two characteristics were particularly good indicators of the lack of financial prudence in the past — the use of state and local debt for essentially private purposes and a continuing deficit in the current account of the governmental unit. Other pertinent characteristics, such as the ability of government officials and the use of budgeting techniques, are very difficult to assess.

Historically, the state and local units which had exercised financial prudence were also usually willing to pay their debt service charges if this was

[16]Information on state and local expenditures were taken from reports by the Governments Division of the Bureau of the Census. Tables 11 and 12 (pp. 63 and 64, respectively) show the proportionate amount of state and local expenditures by character and by purpose in selected years from 1922 through 1968.

possible. Once state and local officials had resorted to poor financial practices, however, the residents and officials of such units often were unwilling to pay their debt service charges. This unwillingness to pay was particularly noticeable in the case of debt-financed projects for essentially private purposes. As long as the bank, canal, railroad, real estate development or other project was successful there was no problem. If the project became unsuccessful, however, the state and local unit was usually either unable or unwilling to pay the debt service charges. Population characteristics, tax collection records, past debt payment performances, maturity schedules and voter approval for debt issues also have been found to indicate the willingness of state and local units to pay their debt service charges.

Analysis of Cross Sections of Available Instrument and Borrower Characteristics

In both major default periods and individual default situations in less extreme periods, debt service charges rose more rapidly than the local levels of income and wealth. The default usually did not occur until after the cash inflows of the unit fell. In individual default situations the local decline in cash inflows may have been caused by the failure of debt-financed private or local enterprises, the collapse of a local real estate boom or the decline of an industry or company on which the community was heavily dependent.

Analysis of cross-sectional data for the 1929 period substantiates the importance of the relationship between debt outstanding, a surrogate for debt service charges, and selected wealth measures indicating potential revenues. Table 8 shows population growth from 1922 to 1932 was more rapid for the eight states where defaulting governmental units numbered 200 or more and the default situation was a serious statewide problem. This growth in population apparently led to even greater demands for debt-financed services. For the eight states with very serious default problems, per capita net debt increased from $89.94 in 1922 to $170.99 in 1932, an increase of 90.1 per cent. For all forty-eight states per capita net debt increased 77.3 per cent, although for the eight states with no default situations in 1935 per capita net debt increased only 51.7 per cent. Net debt per $1,000 of assessed value increased much more rapidly from 1922 to 1932 for the eight states with the most serious debt problems than for the average of all states. By 1932 the net debt per $1,000 of assessed value for the eight states with serious default problems was more than twice the size of this figure for eight states with no defaults in 1935.

The default record of the 190 cities with populations of over 50,000 in 1930 illustrates the effect of the growth in debt relative to population in individual cities. None of the nineteen cities with indebtedness of less than

$50 per capita in 1935 had any serious difficulty in meeting debt require-
ments. All of the nineteen cities with debts of over $200 per capita in 1935
had financial problems. Eight of these nineteen cities were in default during
the depression; five were forced to engage in extensive refinancing operations
to avoid default; three others met their maturing obligations partially by the
issuance of refunding bonds; and the remaining three cities felt the pinch of

TABLE 8

Changes in Per Capita Net Debt and in Net Debt Per Thousand Dollars
of Assessed Valuation, 1922-32

States	Per Capita Net Debt			Net Debt Per $1,000 of Assessed Valuation		
	1932	1922	Per Cent Increase	1932	1922	Per Cent Increase
States with serious default problems						
Arkansas	$137.20	$ 51.03	168.8	$461.18	$157.80	192.2
Florida	357.74	95.96	252.0	985.73	233.17	322.7
Louisana	169.05	69.18	144.4	216.32	81.30	166.1
Michigan	157.66	94.09	67.6	94.68	61.01	55.2
New Jersey	278.61	116.40	139.4	168.81	93.16	81.2
North Carolina	164.84	69.03	138.8	188.21	72.48	159.7
Ohio	129.89	112.25	15.7	64.38	64.33	.1
Texas	125.93	73.71	70.8	176.44	105.36	67.5
Weighted Average	170.99	89.94	90.1	136.09	78.50	73.4
States with no defaults in 1935						
Connecticut	$ 98.59	$ 70.33	40.2	$ 51.00	$ 51.43	d
Delaware	121.20	98.32	23.3	99.56	98.86	.7
Maryland	158.28	81.43	94.4	94.57	71.76	31.8
Massachusetts	101.77	82.30	23.7	58.66	57.59	1.9
New Hampshire	67.81	36.16	87.5	46.70	26.09	79.0
Rhode Island	158.55	79.38	99.7	76.26	47.04	62.1
Vermont	75.50	34.03	121.9	61.64	39.03	57.9
West Virginia	86.33	46.58	85.3	80.72	33.69	139.6
Weighted Average	108.96	71.83	51.7	66.79	53.03	26.0
For all 48 states	141.17	79.90	77.3	107.63	69.71	54.4

Sources: Bureau of the Census, *Financial Statistics of State and Local Governments,
1932* and *Public Debt,* Washington, D.C., 1932 and 1924 respectively.

d = slight percentage decline

deferred commercial bills and payless paydays in order to meet their debt requirements on time.[17]

The ratio of over-all net debt to estimated full taxable property valuation appeared to be a significant indicator of defaults. Forty-nine of the 190 cities with population over 50,000 had a ratio of 9.9 per cent or over in 1935. Only two of these forty-nine cities were free of default, refunding of maturing bonds or funding of deficits during the 1927-37 depression period. Fourteen of these cities defaulted on their general obligation bonds and two had delays classed as technical defaults. Five more defaulted on limited obligation special assessment debt. Seven refunded maturing bonds and issued refunding bonds to take up deficits or finance relief expenditures, seven more refunded maturing bonds (including at least one forced refunding by exchange), and another twelve issued funding bonds for deficit or relief financing or both. Nine of the cities had over-all net debts of 15 per cent or more of full taxable property value. Seven of these nine cities defaulted on their bonds, the eighth refunded maturing bonds and funded deficits and the ninth funded relief expenses. The forty-nine cities with over-all net-debt-to-taxable-property ratio of 9.9 per cent or more accounted for two-thirds of the bond defaults in the 190 city group, and they accounted for all of the situations with protracted difficulties.[18]

The author used three multivariable statistical techniques — factor analysis, multiple discriminate analysis and multiple regression — to analyze the quantitative characteristics associated with the payment or nonpayment of debt service charges by twenty-four Michigan cities in the early 1930's.[19] The quantitative characteristics available for this sample were: dollar amount of notes outstanding, population, total assessed property values, dollar amount of taxes levied, tax levy for $1,000 of assessed value, dollar amount of debt outstanding, per capita debt, debt to assessed property values, per cent of current taxes delinquent, tax levy per capita and assessed property values per capita. The population figures were from 1930 census, the assessed values were for the 1932-33 fiscal year and the remaining measures were as of July 1933.

The factor analysis identified four potential groupings of the eleven quantitative characteristics: (1) size characteristics; (2) debt burden measures, debt

[17]Frederick L. Bird, "Cities and Their Debt Burden," *National Municipal Review*, XXV, No. 1 (January 1936), pp. 12-19.

[18]The figures are based on unpublished information obtained from Dun and Bradstreet.

[19]The author was unable to obtain adequate quantitative information for a larger or broader sample of state and local units in this period. The gathering of the information on the twenty-four Michigan cities and the ensuing statistical analysis were financed by a grant from the Relm Foundation of Ann Arbor, Michigan.

to assessed valuation and debt to population; (3) relative wealth and tax measures, and (4) measures of willingness to pay, such as the tax delinquency rate and the relative tax levy. Because of complications in interpreting the results of factor analysis, these results were primarily used to select the most meaningful combinations of variables for use in further multivariate analysis.

Several different high and low default classes were used with multiple discriminate analysis. The discriminate function between the seven cities with no defaults on their indebtedness in the 1929-37 period and the seventeen cities with one or more issues in default during the same period seemed most meaningful on conceptual grounds and provided the most meaningful results. The most impressive discriminate analysis results occurred when four characteristics — tax rate per $1,000 assessed valuation, tax delinquency rate, assessed property value per capita and either debt to assessed property values or per capita debt — were used. None of the characteristics was almost a linear combination of the other characteristics, three of the four characteristics were significant at the $p > .10$ level (using the t test) and the probability that the discriminate function was due to chance was a relatively low 4 per cent. The confusion matrix (assuming equal a priori probabilities and equal costs) indicated that there were three misclassifications between the defaulting and nondefaulting groups.

The highest proportion of total debt outstanding that was in default in the 1929-37 period was used as the dependent variable in the multiple regression analysis. Using only the variables that were significant at the $p > .075$ level, the linear regression equation explained approximately 64 per cent of the observed differences in the municipalities' default ratios. Using several combinations of only four variables (to restrict multicollinearity), the coefficients of the independent variables were consistent with the conceptual model and the resulting equations explained 40-50 per cent of the observed differences in the default ratios. The characteristics (independent variables) that were used in the preceding regression equations included the five variables which were particularly meaningful in the discriminate analysis and the tax levy per capita.

When multicollinearity is restricted, the variables in both the discriminate analysis and the multiple regression seem consistent with the conceptual model formulated in Chapter 2 of this study. Debt to assessed property values (or per capita debt) would seem to be a meaningful proxy for the relationship between debt service charges and the revenues available to meet these charges. Assessed property values per capita and the property tax levy per $1,000 of assessed property value should indicate the relative wealth of the unit and the extent to which the municipal government is tapping this wealth. These characteristics should improve the quality of the debt to assessed property value or population ratio. The tax delinquency rate and the tax levy per capita would seem to enter into the conceptual model as tests of the financial prudence and willingness to pay of the municipal government and its constituents.

Summary

Both aggregate time series data and cross-sectional analysis of historical instrument and borrower characteristics support the conceptual model developed in Chapter 2. The amount of debt outstanding, a surrogate for debt service charges increased rapidly before each of the four major default periods and prior to many individual default situations. Wealth and income measures, which are indicative of potential cash inflows, appear to have risen less rapidly than estimated debt service charges prior to default periods and situations. These measures then declined absolutely in the economic decline immediately preceding each of the four major default periods. Cash outlays to be paid prior to debt service charges failed to decline as rapidly as cash inflows. Finally, the use of state and local debt for essentially private purposes and a continuing deficit in the current account preceded both major default periods and many individual default situations.

5

POSTWAR TRENDS IN AGGREGATE CHARACTERISTICS AFFECTING QUALITY

The major measurable determinants of the prospective quality of state and local debt may be found by examining instrument and borrower characteristics. The primary purpose of this chapter is to present those instrument and borrower characteristics that the economist, rating agency, etc., can use to assess quality. It is for the person assessing the quality to determine the significance of the level of and changes in these characteristics and the effects of the future external environment. Available, quantifiable characteristics are emphasized; however, pertinent nonquantifiable characteristics are discussed and other useful characteristics are suggested. While postwar data are stressed, characteristics in earlier periods, when available, are presented for comparison.[1] A brief evaluation of the significance of the postwar levels and changes in these characteristics is presented at the end of the chapter. Pertinent instrument and borrower characteristics for several meaningful classifications of state and local debt are examined in the following chapter.

[1]There is obviously no base period which is not subject to criticism as being atypical. Many of the characteristics which the author examines were periodically compiled starting in the years immediately following World War II. Because state and local borrowing was often postponed during World War II and because the economy was extraordinarily liquid in the immediate postwar period, available characteristics from earlier periods are presented for comparison and the atypical nature of the immediate postwar period is recognized in the analysis.

CHART 4
Amounts of State and Local Debt Outstanding and Issued Annually, 1948-68

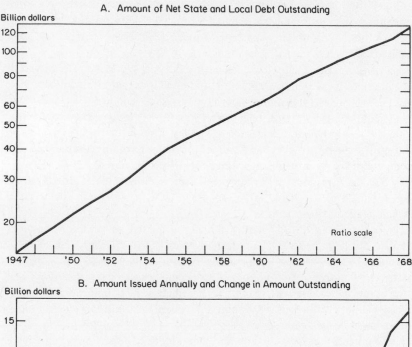

A. Amount of Net State and Local Debt Outstanding

Billion dollars

Ratio scale

B. Amount Issued Annually and Change in Amount Outstanding

Billion dollars

Long-term debt issued

Change in gross amount outstanding

Source: Data in Appendix Tables 1 and 2.

Debt Service Charges in the Postwar Period

The first variable in our model indicating the quality of state and local debt is the amount of debt service charges. While exact figures on debt service charges are not available, some useful estimates can be made. The postwar amounts of state and local debt outstanding, presented here for selected years, are often used as a surrogate for debt service charges. Postwar patterns in maturities and interest costs for state and local debt are discussed. Estimates of the total amount of state and local debt service charges are then presented.

One of the most noticeable trends during the post-World War II period has been the rapid growth in the amount of state and local debt outstanding. The rapid growth in the net amount (excluding issues held by state and local governmental units and their agencies) of state and local debt outstanding during the postwar period is traced on semilog scale in the upper portion of Chart 4. The amount of net state and local debt outstanding has increased at a compound yearly rate of approximately 10 per cent from 1947 through 1968. Net state and local debt grew much more rapidly – albeit from a lower base – than total net debt, total net public debt, or total net private debt throughout the postwar period.[2]

The bottom portion of Chart 4 shows the annual amount of long-term state and local debt issued and the yearly change in the amount of debt outstanding. Despite larger long-term debt retirements (due to the increased amount outstanding), the volume of state and local debt outstanding has grown by an increasing amount. The approximately $7 billion average annual increase in the 1960's is nearly double the roughly $4 billion average annual increase in the early 1950's.

The increasing amount of state and local debt outstanding may not be a very meaningful proxy for debt service charges if the maturity schedules or interest costs of such debt have changed appreciably. The top portion of Chart 5 shows that the cumulative maturities scheduled for long-term state and local debt outstanding shortened slightly between 1941 and 1957, then remained relatively constant through 1962. The bottom portion of the chart demonstrates that the average maturities of long-term state and local debt issued annually remained relatively constant between 1957 and 1968. Thus, it may safely be assumed that the amount of long-term debt maturing annually will probably continue to range between 4 and 5 per cent of the total long-term debt outstanding for at least the next few years.

The interest cost of state and local debt has moved upward in the postwar period. At the present time the average interest cost of all state and local debt

[2]Based on data to be found in Appendix Table 4.

CHART 5
Proportionate Maturity Schedules

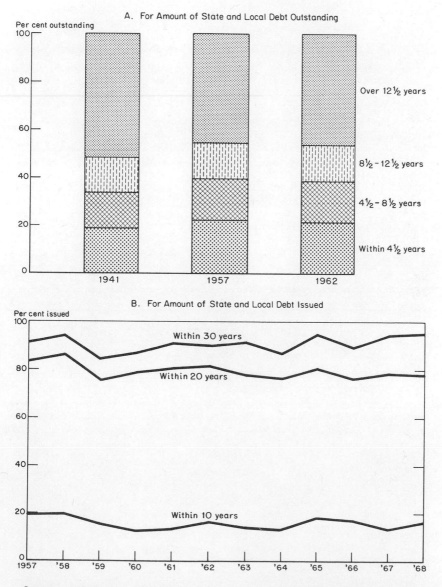

A. For Amount of State and Local Debt Outstanding

Per cent outstanding

Over 12½ years

8½ – 12½ years

4½ – 8½ years

Within 4½ years

1941   1957   1962

B. For Amount of State and Local Debt Issued

Per cent issued

Within 30 years

Within 20 years

Within 10 years

1957 '58 '59 '60 '61 '62 '63 '64 '65 '66 '67 '68

Sources: U.S. Bureau of the Census, *State and Local Government Debt: 1941; Compendium of Government Finances, 1957*; and *Compendium of Government Finances, 1962.* Unpublished data obtained from the Investment Bankers Association.

TABLE 9

Estimated State and Local Debt Service Charges, 1948-68
(in millions of dollars)

Year	Interest on All State and Local Debt	Long-Term Debt Retired	Long-Term Debt Refunded	Interest plus Est. Long-Term Principal Charges[a]	Short-Term Debt Issued	Est. Total Debt Service Charges[b]
1968	3,889	6,002	138	9,753	8,659	18,412
1967	3,634	5,886	174	9,346	8,025	17,371
1966	3,268	5,641	221	8,688	6,523	15,211
1965	3,012	5,040	789	7,263	6,537	13,800
1964	2,826	5,045	657	7,214	5,423	12,637
1963	2,653	4,643	1,277	6,019	5,481	11,500
1962	2,424	4,227	261	6,390	4,763	11,153
1961	2,225	3,696	54	5,867	4,513	10,380
1960	2,028	3,458	53	5,433	4,006	9,439
1959	1,740	3,222	59	4,903	4,179	9,082
1958	1,537	2,839	143	4,233	3,910	8,143
1957	1,376	2,716	60	4,023	3,274	7,306
1956	1,220	2,315	75	3,460	2,706	6,166
1955	1,059	2,351	76	3,334	2,593	5,927
1954	916	2,327	158	3,085	3,350	6,435
1953	797	1,982	127	2,652	2,757	5,409
1952	724	1,747	330	2,141	2,049	4,190
1951	647	1,278	98	1,827	1,637	3,464
1950	613	1,178	122	1,669	1,611	3,280
1949	578	822	105	1,295	1,333	2,628
1948	543	1,113	187	1,469	1,005	2,747

Sources: Interest figures from U.S. Department of Commerce, *Historical Statistician on Governmental Finances,* Vol. VI, No. 4 of *1962 Census of Governments;* and *Summary of Governmental Finances* in 1965-68. Other figures from records of *The Daily Bond Buyer.*

[a]Interest plus long-term debt retired in period less long-term debt refunded.

[b]Interest plus estimated long-term principal charges plus all short-term debt issued.

outstanding is slightly above 3 per cent. This interest cost will probably continue to increase since the marginal interest rate exceeded 5 per cent in the mid-1960's.

Because of the rapid increase in the amounts of debt outstanding, the relatively constant maturity schedules and the increasing average interest costs, it is evident that state and local debt service charges increased rapidly in the postwar period. Table 9 shows estimated state and local debt service

CHART 6
Debt Service Charge Measures as a Per Cent of Debt Outstanding, 1948-68

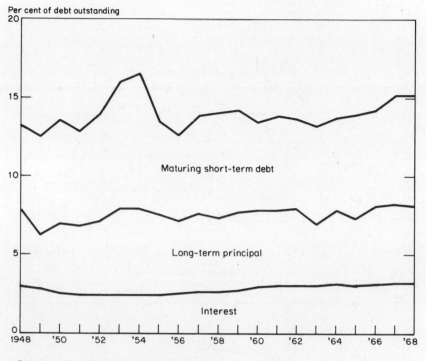

Per cent of debt outstanding

Maturing short-term debt

Long-term principal

Interest

Sources: Table 9 and Appendix Table 1.

charges from 1948 through 1968. The long-term debt retired annually (except through refunding) was added to the interest on all state and local debt to estimate the interest plus long-term principal charges. The dollar amount of short-term debt issued during the year was then added to this figure to obtain estimated total debt service charges.

Chart 6 shows that the resulting debt service charge measures, although very rough estimates, have been a remarkably stable per cent of total debt outstanding from 1948 through 1968. This reasonably stable relationship indicates that, when properly used, state and local debt outstanding is a meaningful proxy for the service charges on such debt.

Over-all State and Local Cash Inflows

The model developed in the preceding chapters indicated that the ability to meet debt service charges was a function of the relation of such charges to the

CHART 7
Debt Service Charge Measures as a Per Cent of State and Local General Revenues, 1948-68

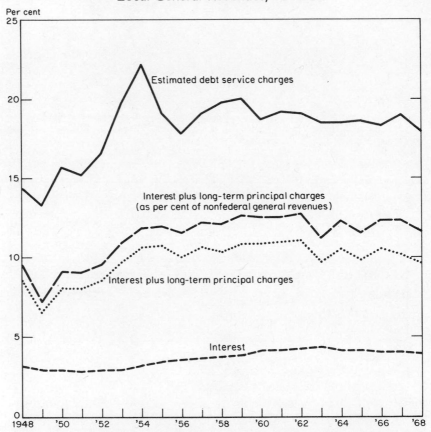

Per cent

Sources: Table 10: Governments Division, U.S. Bureau of the Census, *Historical Statistics on Government Finances,* Vol. VI, No. 4 of *1962 Census of Governments;* and *Governmental Finances,* 1965-68 issues.

difference between the potential over-all cash inflows and cash outflows having priority over the charges. The direct relationships between debt service costs and over-all state and local general revenues[3] appears in Chart 7. This chart shows that interest costs rose from under 3 per cent of general revenues in the late 1940's and early 1950's to slightly over 4 per cent in the early and mid-1960's. Interest costs plus net long-term retirements rose from around 8

[3]State and local general revenues are all state and local revenue except utility and liquor-store revenues and insurance-trust revenues.

per cent to above 10 per cent of general revenues during the same period. Estimated total debt service charges as a proportion of general revenues were under 15 per cent in the late 1940's but increased over 18 per cent in the early and mid-1960's. Two other observations can be made from this chart. First, the rate of increase in debt service charges as a percentage of general revenues has slowed in recent years. Second, if federal government aid is removed from state and local general revenues, the increases in debt service charges as a percentage of state and local revenues have been more pronounced.

Estimates of debt service charges prior to the postwar period were available for only three years: 1922, 1927 and 1932. In 1922 and 1927 interest was approximately 9 per cent of general revenues, interest plus net maturing long-term debt was 13-15 per cent of general revenues, and estimated debt service cost was 22-24 per cent. Debt service costs continued to rise into the 1930's while general revenues declined slightly; therefore, debt service charges were a much higher percentage of state and local general revenues in 1932.[4]

Before turning to the cash outlays which will be paid before debt service charges, the sources of over-all state and local cash inflows should be examined. The major sources of state and local general revenues changed appreciably between the pre- and early post-World War II periods (see Table 10). Most of these changes continued at a more moderate pace throughout the postwar period. Most noticeable are the decreases in the proportionate amounts of property taxes and license fees (most of the other taxes category) and the proportionate increases in receipts from sales and income taxes and fiscal aid from the federal government. The changing nature of proportionate sources of state and local revenues help indicate the prospective reliability of cash inflows and help indentify the significant underlying resources.

Reliability implies dependability even under trying economic or social conditions. In the preceding chapters, it was indicated that the general property tax had been one of the most reliable sources of tax revenues during trying times. Even in depression periods when tax payments lagged behind schedule, it was generally possible to borrow against delinquent property taxes. Specific sales taxes on consumer necessities, excise taxes and most licenses also appear to be reliable, although they tend to fluctuate somewhat with economic prosperity. Income taxes, general sales taxes and general revenue taxes seem to be most vulnerable to economic fluctuations.

Based on these generalizations, the contemporary scene is far more complex than the situation prior to the 1929 state and local debt default period. The sources of state and local revenues have become more diversified and the

[4]Revenue figures and interest costs from Bureau of the Census, U. S. Department of Commerce. Long-term principal charges and amount of short-term debt issued obtained from *The Daily Bond Buyer*.

TABLE 10

Selected General Revenue Items as a Percentage of
General State and Local Revenues, 1922-68

Year	General Revenues ($ billions)	Percentage Distribution					
		Property Taxes	Sales Taxes[a]	Income Taxes[b]	Other Taxes[c]	Fiscal Aid[d]	Misc. General Revenues
1968	101.3	27.4	22.6	9.7	7.0	17.0	16.3
1967	91.6	28.7	22.5	8.8	6.9	16.9	16.2
1966	83.0	29.7	23.0	8.2	7.5	15.8	15.9
1965	74.0	30.5	23.1	8.1	7.5	14.9	15.9
1964	68.4	31.0	23.0	8.0	7.7	14.6	15.6
1963	62.3	31.9	23.2	7.7	8.0	13.9	15.4
1962	58.2	32.7	23.2	7.5	8.0	13.5	15.2
1961	54.0	33.3	23.1	7.2	8.4	13.2	14.9
1960	50.5	32.5	23.5	7.2	8.4	13.8	14.7
1959	45.3	33.1	23.0	6.6	8.8	14.1	14.5
1958	41.2	34.1	23.8	6.7	9.0	11.8	14.5
1957	38.2	33.7	24.8	7.2	9.8	10.1	14.4
1956	34.7	33.9	25.1	7.0	10.1	9.6	14.3
1955	31.1	34.5	24.6	6.4	10.1	10.1	14.4
1954	29.0	34.4	25.1	6.6	10.1	10.2	13.7
1953	27.3	34.3	25.4	6.9	10.0	10.5	12.9
1952	25.2	34.4	25.2	7.3	9.8	10.2	13.1
1950	20.9	35.1	24.6	6.6	9.7	11.9	12.0
1948	17.3	35.5	25.8	6.6	9.5	10.8	11.9
1946	12.4	40.4	24.2	7.0	10.1	6.9	11.4
1940	9.6	46.1	20.6	4.0	10.6	9.8	8.9
1936	8.4	48.8	17.7	3.2	10.2	11.3	8.9
1932	7.3	61.7	10.3	2.1	10.6	3.2	12.0
1927	7.3	65.1	6.5	2.2	10.0	1.6	14.7
1922	4.8	69.5	3.2	2.1	9.2	2.3	13.7

Sources: U.S. Department of Commerce, *Historical Statistics on Governmental Finances,* Vol. IV, No. 4 of *1962 Census of Governments;* and *Governmental Finances in 1965-68.*

[a]Includes general and specific sales taxes and gross receipts taxes.

[b]Includes business and personal income taxes.

[c]Most of these taxes are motor vehicle licenses and registration fees and operators license.

[d]Aid from the federal government to state and local governmental units.

CHART 8
Selected Aggregative Measures of the State and Local Debt Burden, 1947-68

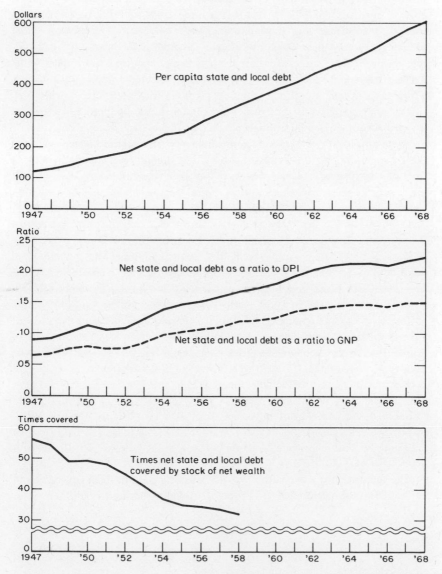

Sources: Data in the top panel is from the U.S. Bureau of the Census. Data in the middle and bottom panels are from Appendix Table 4.

increase in fiscal aid (both federal aid to states and state aid to local units) should help financially weak units. On the other hand, the relative decline in the previously dependable property taxes and license receipts and the proportionate increase in revenues based on cyclically vulnerable income and consumption may make state and local cash inflows more rather than less vulnerable to cyclical economic disturbances. Even fiscal aid, the fastest growing source of state and local revenues in the postwar period, is suspect. Most federal taxes are vulnerable to declines in income and consumption.[5] Nearly two-thirds of state and local cash inflows including fiscal aid appear to be derived from taxes and other revenues based on income and consumption. Thus, the shifts in the primary sources of cash inflows seem to indicate that, *ceteris paribus,* relatively more general revenues should be required to support a given level of state and local debt.

State and local cash flows depend on the growth of the tax base and the tax-paying ability of their constituents. While the tax base is partially a function of the type of tax assessed, both the base and tax-paying ability must ultimately be paid from the wealth, production and income of our economy. Chart 8 demonstrates the relationship between state and local debt outstanding, a surrogate for debt service charges, and the population, Gross National Product and Disposable Personal Income in the United States from 1947 through 1968. The chart also reveals the number of times that net state and local debt is covered by the stock of net wealth of the United States from 1947-58. Chart 8 discloses that per capita state and local debt increased from $119 in 1947 to $606 in 1968. During the same period, the ratio of net state and local debt outstanding to GNP rose from .065 to .149 and the ratio of debt to DPI rose from .088 to .218. In the 1947-58 period, the coverage of net state and local debt by the stock of net debt fell; in 1947 net wealth was 54.2 times the net debt, in 1958 wealth was 32 times debt.[6]

It is pertinent to observe what happened to most of these same measures prior to the most recent major default period, the 1929 depression era. The amount of per capita debt increased from $65 in 1918 to $130 in 1928. During the same period the ratio of net debt to GNP increased from .076 to .129 and the coverage of net debt by net wealth fell from 62.9 times to 34.9 times.[7]

The relationship between the over-all debt of a state or local governmental unit and the total estimated full property values in that unit is another useful

[5]This vulnerability is limited by the ability and willingness of the federal government to use deficit financing.

[6]For yearly figures see Appendix Tables 2 and 4. Per capita figures are based on the population estimates of the Bureau of the Census.

[7]*Ibid.*

CHART 9
Median Over-All Tax-Supported Debt to Estimated Full Property Valuation for 200 Largest U.S. Cities, 1947-68

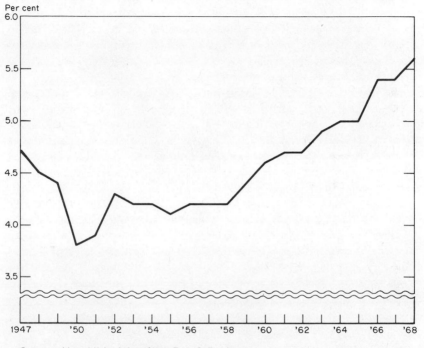

Source: Unpublished data from Dun & Bradstreet.

comparison. Estimated true property values are primarily a proxy for wealth, but also may be indicative of the property tax base. Chart 9 shows that the ratio of the median over-all taxable debt to estimated true property values for the 200 largest U. S. cities rose from less than 3 per cent in the late 1940's to more than 5 per cent in the mid-1960's. The median for the same ratio for the 190 largest U. S. cities had been slightly above 7 per cent in 1935. The decidedly faster growth of estimated full property values relative to debt was a significant indicator of defaults in the last major default period.[8]

Resources Available to Pay Debt Service Charges

The discussion so far has emphasized the relationship between debt service

[8]Based on unpublished information obtained from Dun and Bradstreet. The past performance of the debt to estimated true property value relationship was discussed on pages .

charges and gross state and local revenues and the resources underlying these revenues. The relationship between debt service charges and the resources available to pay those charges is conceptually much more meaningful. It is very difficult, however, to estimate the resources available to meet debt service charges. Three aspects, plus the previously discussed over-all cash inflows, are significant in determining the resources available to pay debt service charges: the flexibility in the use of state and local revenues; the estimated cash outlays that will be made prior to debt service charges; and the cash and near cash balances available to meet the charges.

The importance of flexibility in the use of revenues was demonstrated during the last major default period. In that period the revenues of some governmental units were sufficient, but the mechanics of their allocation prevented application where needed. Despite the demonstrated importance of flexibility, it seems that the debt structure and revenue system are more rigid today than they were during the 1929-33 depression period or even in the years immediately following World War II.

Two state and local financial techniques appear to be reducing the flexibility of state and local revenue systems. The first of these is earmarking. In earmarking liens are placed on certain revenues or fractions of revenues in favor of a particular series of general obligations. This may be accomplished either by legislative fiat or by contract with bondholders. There are few details about the amount of earmarking in the 1920's and early 1930's, but the practice then appears to have been rudimentary by present standards and limited primarily to highway-user taxes. Today, however, earmarking is a common practice in many governmental units and extends to most of the major segments of the state and local revenue system.[9]

The second financial technique reducing the flexibility in revenue systems is the use of certain designated revenues and can be distinguished from the full faith and credit pledged by similar issuers of general obligations.[10] These bonds are payable solely from limited liability obligations. The revenues from which limited liability obligations are to be paid are usually restricted solely for this use. Therefore, even if the designated revenues (which the Bureau of the Census classifies as general revenues) are several times the debt service

---

[9]Evidence of the widespread use of earmarking in the postwar period appears in: Tax Foundation, Inc., *Earmarked State Taxes,* Project No. 38, New York, 1964; and Citizens Research Council of Michigan, *Earmarking of Tax Revenues,* Detroit, 1962.

[10]Nearly all of the limited obligations of state and local units are conventionally called "revenue bonds." The U. S. Bureau of the Census uses the term "non-guaranteed debt" to represent the limited liability obligations of state and local units. Non-guaranteed debt includes limited liability special assessment bonds, whereas, these bonds are not included in the conventional revenue bond category. However, because of the small amount of special assessment bonds outstanding or recently issued, the terms revenue bonds and non-guaranteed debt are used interchangeably to describe the limited liability obligations of state and local governments.

CHART 10
Proportionate Amount of Limited Liability Obligations Issued and Outstanding During the Postwar Period, 1947-68

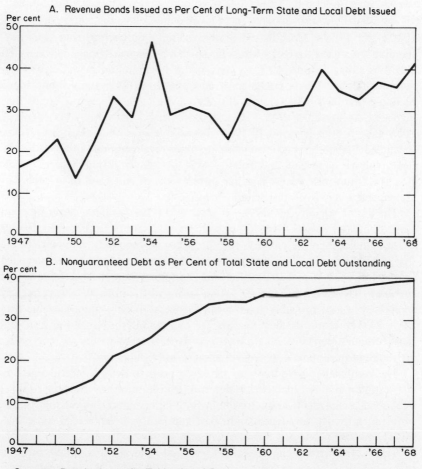

A. Revenue Bonds Issued as Per Cent of Long-Term State and Local Debt Issued

B. Nonguaranteed Debt as Per Cent of Total State and Local Debt Outstanding

Sources: Data in Appendix Tables 1 and 2.

requirements, the revenues remaining after debt service charges are paid cannot be used for other purposes.

The top portion of Chart 10 shows that limited liability bonds have been an increasing portion of long-term state and local debt issued during the postwar period, representing over one-fourth of such debt issued in all but one of the years since 1952. Similar historical data in Appendix Table 1 reveal that revenue bonds had always accounted for less than 10 per cent prior to 1943. The combined information from Chart 10 and Appendix Table 1 demonstrates the long and more or less steady increase in reliance on

revenue bonds and the commensurate decline in reliance on general obligations throughout the postwar period.

This trend has increased the relative amount of limited liability debt outstanding while lessening that of general obligations outstanding. Historical
data in Appendix Table 2 suggest that limited liability obligations accounted
for less than one-ninth of state and local debt outstanding throughout the
1920's and 1930's. Most of the limited liability obligations that were outstanding up to the early 1930's were special assessment bonds.[11] Chart 10
also shows that in 1948, 10.3 per cent of the dollar amount of state and local
debt outstanding was in non-guaranteed obligations. The relative importance
of non-guaranteed debt (almost entirely in the form of revenue bonds) has
increased rapidly since 1948 — rising to 34.2 per cent of total indebtedness in
1958 and to 39.3 per cent in 1968. Because general obligations are usually
scheduled for more rapid retirement than are revenue bonds and because the
heavy volume of revenue bonds issued will probably continue, it seems likely
that the future will see even higher proportions of state and local debt that
are payable solely from designated revenues.

The greater rigidity in the use of state and local revenues, resulting from
earmarking and revenue-dedication, might create serious problems in periods
of declining economic activity and declining government revenues. If the
degree of earmarking and revenue dedication that exists today had prevailed
during the 1929 depression period, many more state and local debts would
probably have gone into default. Also, many difficulties that were merely
temporary would probably have swelled to chronic and unmanageable proportions. Therefore, the declining degree of flexibility in the use of state and
local revenues seem to indicate that, *ceteris paribus,* relatively more revenues
are required to support a given level of state and local debt.

The estimated cash outlays to be made prior to debt service charges are
the second major consideration in determining the resources available to meet
debt service charges. No directly quantifiable information is available on this
problem, although an understanding of the nature of state and local cash
outlays gives some insights into the problem.

Table 11 illustrates the proportion of total general expenditures spent in
major functional areas in selected years from 1922—68. The information on
this table indicates that educational expenditures have grown in relative importance and constituted approximately 40 per cent of total general expenditures by the mid-1960's. Roads and highways, the second highest functional
expenditure, have declined in proportional importance from about one-fourth

[11]It is estimated that the proportionate dollar amount of revenue bonds to total state
and local indebtedness was .5 per cent in 1925, 2 per cent in 1931 and 5 per cent in
1937. It is estimated that limited liability special assessment bonds were 6—7 per cent
of total state and local indebtedness in the late 1920's. However, an extremely low dollar
amount of limited liability special assessment bonds was issued after the 1929 depression
period.

TABLE 11

State and Local General Expenditures Classified by Major Function for Selected Years 1922-68

Year	General Expenditures ($ billions)	Percentage Distribution				
		Education	Roads & Highway	Public Welfare	Health & Hospitals	Protection & Sanitation
1968	102.4	40.2	14.1	9.6	7.5	7.7
1967	93.8	40.8	14.9	8.8	7.2	7.9
1966	82.8	40.2	15.4	8.2	7.1	8.1
1965	74.5	38.3	16.4	8.5	7.2	8.3
1964	69.3	37.9	16.8	8.4	7.1	8.4
1963	64.0	37.1	17.4	8.5	7.2	8.4
1962	60.2	36.9	17.2	8.4	7.2	8.7
1961	56.2	36.6	17.5	8.4	7.3	8.7
1960	50.9	36.1	18.2	8.5	7.3	8.8
1959	48.9	35.4	19.6	8.5	7.6	8.7
1958	44.9	35.7	19.1	8.5	7.7	8.9
1957	40.4	35.0	19.4	8.6	7.7	9.2
1956	36.7	36.0	18.9	8.6	7.6	9.2
1955	33.7	35.3	19.1	9.4	7.5	9.1
1954	30.7	34.4	18.0	10.0	7.8	9.1
1953	27.9	33.6	17.9	10.4	8.2	9.1
1952	26.1	31.9	17.8	10.7	8.4	9.7
1950	22.8	31.5	16.7	12.9	7.7	9.2
1948	17.7	30.4	17.2	11.9	6.9	9.7
1946	11.0	30.4	15.2	12.8	7.4	10.4
1940	9.2	28.6	17.0	12.5	6.6	8.7
1936	7.6	28.5	18.6	10.8	6.1	9.5
1932	7.8	29.8	22.4	5.7	5.9	9.7
1927	7.2	31.0	25.1	2.1	4.9	10.9
1922	5.2	32.7	24.7	2.2	4.9	10.3

Sources: U.S. Department of Commerce, *Historical Statistics on Governmental Finances,* Vol. IV, No. 4 of *1962 Census of Governments;* and *Summary of Governmental Finances in 1965-68.*

[a]Functions were 5 per cent or more of the total.

TABLE 12

Amount of State and Local Expenditures, by Character,
Selected Years, 1922-68
(amounts in millions of dollars)

Year	Expenditures	Current Operations		Capital Outlays		Assistance and Subsidies	
		Amount	% of Total	Amount	% of Total	Amount	% of Total
1968	116,245	75,311	64.8	25,731	22.1	5,659	4.9
1967	106,675	68,248	64.0	24,506	23.0	5,010	4.7
1966	94,906	60,212	63.4	22,330	23.5	4,315	4.5
1965	86,554	53,929	62.3	20,535	23.7	4,127	4.8
1964	80,579	49,687	61.7	19,087	23.7	3,885	4.8
1963	74,698	45,473	60.9	17,637	23.6	3,737	5.0
1962	70,547	42,736	60.6	16,791	23.8	3,708	5.3
1961	67,023	39,800	59.4	16,091	24.0	3,607	5.4
1960	60,999	36,318	59.5	15,104	24.8	3,518	5.8
1959	58,572	33,369	57.0	15,351	26.2	3,329	5.7
1958	53,712	30,862	57.5	13,986	26.0	3,159	5.9
1957	47,553	27,983	58.8	12,616	26.5	2,828	5.9
1956	43,152	25,828	59.9	11,407	26.4	2,620	6.1
1955	40,375	23,186	57.4	10,705	26.5	2,660	6.6
1954	36,607	21,508	58.8	9,125	24.9	2,634	7.2
1953	32,937	19,965	60.6	7,905	24.0	2,558	7.8
1952	30,863	18,533	60.0	7,436	24.1	2,472	8.0
1950	27,905	15,948	57.2	6,047	21.7	2,918	10.5
1948	21,260	13,415	63.1	3,725	17.5	2,381	11.2
1946	14,067	9,690	68.9	1,305	9.3	1,209	8.6
1940	11,240	6,176	54.9	2,515	22.4	1,075	9.6
1936	8,501	5,228	61.5	1,524	17.9	752	8.8
1932	8,403	5,179	61.6	1,876	22.3	388	4.6
1927	7,810	4,590	58.8	2,356	30.2	93	1.2
1922	5,652	3,477	61.5	1,518	26.9	152	2.7

Sources: U.S. Department of Commerce, *Historical Statistics on Governmental Finances,* Vol. IV, No. 4 of *1962 Census of Governments;* and *Summary of Governmental Finances in 1965-68.*

of general expenditures in the 1920's and 1930's to approximately 15 per cent in the mid-1960's. Other categories constituting over 5 per cent of general expenditures in recent years include public welfare, health and hospitals, and protection and sanitation.

Table 12 reveals the proportion of total state and local expenditures for current operations, capital outlays and assistance and subsidies. In spite of severe financial problems in the early 1930's, current operating expenditures continued to rise; however, capital outlays declined. In recent years the proportionate amount spent on current operations has risen while the propor-

CHART 11
Absolute and Relative Amounts of State and Local Financial Assets, 1946-68

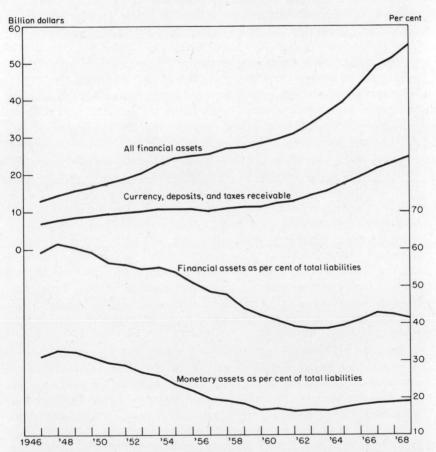

Billion dollars

Per cent

All financial assets

Currency, deposits, and taxes receivable

Financial assets as per cent of total liabilities

Monetary assets as per cent of total liabilities

Sources: Goldsmith, Raymond W., Lipsey, Robert E., and Mendelson, Morris, *Studies in the National Balance Sheet of the United States,* Vol. II, Princeton for NBER, 1963, Table III-6, pp. 216-217. Recent figures from unpublished FRB worksheets and *Governmental Finances,* 1959-68 issues.

tionate amount spent on capital outlays declined. Expenditures for assistance and subsidies which rose throughout the 1930's have declined as a proportion of total expenditures in the 1950's and early 1960's.

Several additional general observations can be made about the cash outlays with priority over debt service charges. First, state and local expenditures for public welfare and assistance and subsidies will not increase rapidly even if the economy declines, as the federal government has taken over much of this function. These expenditures, however, will probably increase moderately and cannot be expected to decline. Second, the unionization of many state and local employees has increased the rigidity of state and local salaries and wages and may lead to increases in these expenditures even in times of economic slack. Third, state and local units are now legally obligated to sustain essential services and meet employee payrolls before paying debt service charges. In the debt default period during the early 1930's, many state and local governmental units with revenue deficiencies postponed maintenance expense, reduced services and cut employees' salaries in order to meet debt service charges. In the Asbury Park Case (1938) and the Sheffield Case (1948) the courts found that necessary and proper state and local expenses must be paid before debt service charges. These cases would appear to make state and local expenditures substantially more rigid than they were in the 1930's.

The third major consideration in determining the resources available to meet debt service charges is the amount of money and other liquid assets of state and local units that might be available to pay debt service charges. Chart 11 shows the amount of currency, deposits and receivable taxes held by state and local units (excluding pension and retirement fund amounts) and the total amount of financial assets held by these units. Both of these amounts grew absolutely throughout the postwar period. Chart 11 also shows that these cash and financial asset holdings did not grow as fast as the growth in the total liabilities of the units. This relative decline in cash and financial asset holdings was particularly pronounced in the mid- and late 1950's. There was a slight relative recovery in the mid-1960's; however, cash and financial asset holdings relative to financial liabilities did not climb back to the level they held during the mid-1950's.

Because of the inexact measurements of reliable cash inflows, cash outlays to be paid before debt service charges and the proportion of financial assets that could be used to pay debt service charges, any direct comparisons of net cash available to meet debt service charges and debt service charges seems tenuous. Therefore, the comparison presented in Chart 12, while conceptually correct, is tenuous as a quantitative measure. For Chart 12 net cash flows available to meet debt service charges are estimated to be total general revenues less all general expenditures for education, public welfare, health and hospitals, and protection services and less one-half of the remaining general expenditures excluding interest. This net cash flow figure is compared with interest plus estimated long-term principal charges, and then this net cash

CHART 12
Times Estimated Debt Service Charges Are Covered by Estimated Usable Cash Resources, 1948-67

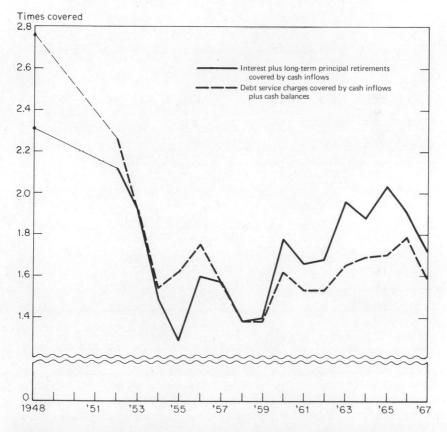

Sources: Debt service charges from Table 9, usable cash balances estimated from Chart 11, estimated usable cash inflows from Chart 7 and Table 11.

flow figure plus one-half of state and local currency, deposits and taxes receivable balances are compared with estimated total debt service charges.[12]

The tentative results of Chart 12 indicate that net cash flows available to meet debt service charges declined relative to debt service charges from 1948

[12]The basis for the expenditure weighting was the fact that the amount of expenditures for education, public welfare, health and hospitals, and protective services have not declined appreciably in any year since 1927. Expenditures for most other functions have tended to decline somewhat, particularly in depression or recession periods. Few, if any, of these remaining expenditures could decline 50 per cent at the present time. Half of the currency, deposit and taxes receivable balances were used to represent the cash balances state and local governments might be able to use to meet debt service charges.

CHART 13
Long-Term State and Local Debt Issued as a Per Cent of

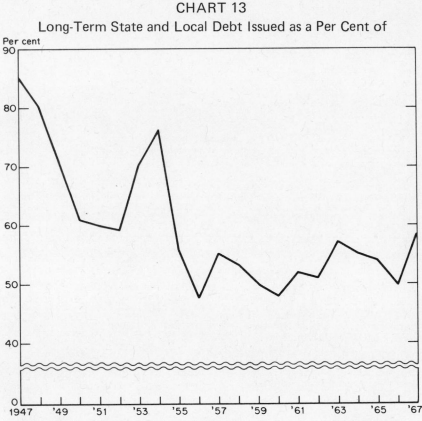

Per cent

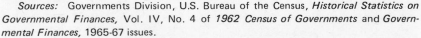

Sources: Governments Division, U.S. Bureau of the Census, *Historical Statistics on Governmental Finances,* Vol. IV, No. 4 of *1962 Census of Governments* and *Governmental Finances,* 1965-67 issues.

through most of the 1950's, then began to increase relative to debt service charges in the early 1960's. The decline in the late 1940's and early 1950's was at least partially caused by the rapid increase from a low level of state and local debt and the relation of the high liquidity of many state and local units in the immediate postwar period. The increase in the early 1960's was caused primarily by the increased liquidity of state and local units and by a decline in the relative importance of public welfare, health and hospitals, and protective services expenditures. In the mid-1960's then conditions were reversed, and net cash flows declined somewhat relative to debt service charges.

Financial Prudence and Willingness to Pay

The last variables in our model indicating the quality of state and local debt are measures appraising the financial prudence and willingness to pay of the

TABLE 13

Purpose of Long-Term State and Local Debt Issued from 1948 through 1968
(expressed as a per cent of annual amount issued)

	Education	Ground Transportation	Ports and Airports	Water and Sewer	Other Utilities	Health and Welfare	Recreation	Industrial	Public Housing	Veterans Aid	Refunding	Other and Unidentified
1948	13.8	14.1	3.6	10.5	4.1	1.2	1.0	.0	4.9	21.5	6.4	18.7
1949	17.5	17.3	2.2	13.3	4.8	1.6	1.2	.0	6.8	8.8	3.6	22.8
1950	19.2	13.8	1.8	13.2	3.6	2.6	.9	2.2	3.3	17.2	3.1	19.1
1951	17.8	17.7	.8	14.2	5.4	4.1	.2	.1	11.0	1.3	2.7	24.6
1952	22.0	21.3	1.4	9.5	5.1	.8	.5	.1	9.6	2.3	7.1	20.3
1953	23.7	28.5	.9	11.6	2.8	2.4	.8	.1	9.1	2.5	1.5	16.0
1954	20.5	30.6	1.3	9.7	8.6	1.1	.8	.0	6.5	2.3	2.6	15.9
1955	25.4	22.8	1.7	11.9	2.8	1.6	.7	.3	9.5	2.8	1.1	19.6
1956	26.7	12.8	2.5	13.8	11.9	1.1	.7	.1	4.7	2.0	1.1	22.3
1957	35.6	15.5	2.7	14.8	7.2	2.0	1.2	.1	1.7	4.9	.7	13.8
1958	34.2	15.7	2.6	14.4	4.2	2.9	1.3	.4	3.4	4.6	1.2	15.1
1959	29.1	11.1	4.7	14.7	11.2	1.5	1.0	.3	5.3	4.7	1.4	15.0
1960	32.0	14.0	4.4	14.5	3.4	1.4	.9	.6	5.9	2.8	.6	19.4
1961	32.2	13.8	3.8	15.4	4.5	1.2	1.7	.7	4.6	5.7	1.2	15.3
1962	32.8	12.8	3.7	13.7	5.1	1.6	1.8	1.0	6.0	1.4	3.2	16.9
1963	27.8	7.9	2.7	13.5	8.6	2.1	1.0	1.2	5.8	.0	13.5	16.0
1964	30.6	6.5	3.6	14.8	7.5	.9	2.0	1.8	6.8	1.1	6.1	18.2
1965	31.3	8.1	2.3	13.0	4.3	1.8	1.4	2.0	5.6	.4	7.7	22.2
1966	31.3	14.1	2.3	13.6	3.1	4.7	1.0	4.5	4.8	.0	.9	19.6
1967	29.5	10.8	3.5	12.9	3.6	5.1	1.0	9.7	4.5	.0	.9	18.5
1968	28.4	13.7	3.7	11.4	5.6	5.1	1.1	9.8	4.8	.0	.7	15.6
1948-68	28.1	14.1	2.8	13.2	5.6	2.4	1.2	2.3	5.6	3.2	3.4	18.1

Sources: Summarized from an unpublished monograph by the Board of Governors of the Federal Reserve System and data from the Investment Bankers Association.

Note: Due to the rounding of individual figures, some of the yearly totals do not add to 100.0 per cent.

borrowing governmental unit. The amazing record of what some state and local governments have done with limited cash inflows relative to their debt service charges and the need to have some assurance as to the good faith and management of the borrowing unit indicate that this category of variables should not be ignored. Four types of measures are examined: the purpose of the indebtedness, the debt retirement arrangements, the voter debt approval record and the revenue collection performance of the governmental unit.

The purpose of state and local indebtedness is generally considered appropriate when the outlay is (1) extraordinarily large and nonrecurring and (2) in the public interest. Postwar policies and practices related to the first of these two requirements appear to be favorable. Table 13 shows that most of the proceeds from the sale of long-term state and local debt during the postwar period have been used to finance capital intensive purposes such as education, roads and bridges, housing and utilities. Chart 13 shows that long-term state and local debt issued has fluctuated between roughly 50 and 60 per cent of state and local capital outlays in the last decade. In addition to supporting the idea of debt being issued for appropriate purposes, the relationship in Chart 13 indicates that, in the aggregate, current cash inflows are covering all state and local current outlays as well as some of their capital outlays. Deficits in the state and local current account had been one of the important historical indicators of individual state and local debt default situations.

The second of these two requirements, borrowing in the public interest, is a highly subjective concept which may change with shifts in conditions and attitudes. It is usually concluded that the use of public credit for essentially private purposes is inappropriate and may lead to serious problems if the private interests involved get in financial difficulties. The use of public credit for essentially private purposes was determined as a cause in all of the four previous major state and local debt default periods.

A review of Table 13 reveals that the only contemporary practice in which state and local debt is used for essentially private purposes is the use of long-term debt proceeds for industrial aid. Typically these industrial aid bonds are issued to build factories for lease to business concerns. Table 13 shows that the amount of long-term state and local debt used for industrial aid has been slightly more than 2 per cent of all long-term state and local issued from 1948 through 1968. While the amount of industrial aid bonds outstanding is still relatively small, state and local debt issued for industrial aid could be a serious trouble spot.[13] Moreover, Table 13 shows that the relative amount of industrial aid bonds issued has grown very rapidly in the mid-1960's.[14]

---

[13]There are five known cases in which the business concern using the plant financed by industrial aid bonds has failed or been forced to leave the site. These five cases are general obligations and the communities involved have made all debt service payments so far. It will be interesting to observe what happens if an industrial aid revenue issue is involved in a similar situation.

CHART 14

Relative Amounts of Long-Term Debt of Special Districts[a] and Local Statutory Authorities[b] Outstanding and Newly Issued in Selected Years

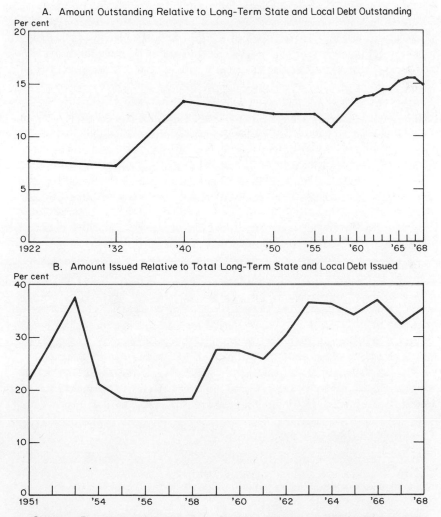

A. Amount Outstanding Relative to Long-Term State and Local Debt Outstanding

B. Amount Issued Relative to Total Long-Term State and Local Debt Issued

Sources: Data in Appendix Tables 1, 2 and 3. Amount of special district and local statutory authority debt issued is from the Investment Bankers Association (for 1957-68 data) and from *Federal Reserve Bulletins* (for 1951-56 data).

[a] Excluding School Districts

[b] Excludes state statutory authorities. In addition, the debt outstanding figure probably excludes some local statutory authorities. Further breakdown of these figures are not available at the present time.

It is also questionable whether the borrowing of some special districts and statutory authorities is in the public interest. Borrowing by these types of political subdivisions often does not require voter approval, is generally not subject to debt restrictions and may conceal the indebtedness from the great mass of voters and taxpayers. Past state and local debt default records have a liberal sprinkling of cases in which the issuing special district or statutory authority has been unable to obtain public support when it has gotten into financial difficulties. The top part of Chart 14 shows that the outstanding amount of long-term debt by special districts other than school districts[15] and local statutory authorities has risen from 7.7 and 7.2 per cent of total long-term state and local debt outstanding in 1922 and 1932 respectively to over 15 per cent of total long-term state and local debt outstanding in the mid-1960's. The lower part of Chart 14 shows that the relative proportion of long-term state and local debt issued by special districts (other than school districts) and local statutory authorities has been increasing in recent years. The bonds of these special districts and local statutory authorities accounted for approximately a third of all long-term state and local debt issued so far in the 1960's. If state statutory authorities were included the proportionate share would be even larger — Table 16 (page 94) shows that state non-guaranteed debt, much of which was statutory authority debt, constituted over half of all state indebtedness outstanding in the 1960's.

The objective here is not to condemn the issuance of all debt by all special districts and statutory authorities. Borrowing by these political subdivisions may be the only method possible when there are unrealistic debt limits or when the debt financed service benefits several governmental units. However, past misuse of borrowing by some special districts and statutory authorities indicates that the increased relative growth in bonds issued by these political subdivisions should be carefully scrutinized for possible financial dangers.

The continuous postwar increase in state and local limited liability obligations, discussed earlier and documented in Chart 10 (page 61), should also be carefully scrutinized. If the limited cash inflows are insufficient to pay the debt service charges on these obligations, many state and local units may be unwilling to support such indebtedness.[16]

[14]After December 31, 1968, the interest on issues of over $1 million of state and local debt issued for industrial aid became subject to the federal income tax. The effect of this legislation will probably be a drastic reduction in the volume of state and local industrial aid bonds issued.

[15]The indebtedness of school districts was not included because such indebtedness is generally not concealed, often requires voter approval and had the lowest over-all incidence of defaults of all political subdivisions in the 1929 depression period.

[16]During the postwar period, some issuing or benefiting government units have aided their limited liability obligations, while others have openly refused to do so. For example, Kansas City, Missouri, advanced supplementary funds so that interest on its Auditorium Plaza Garage revenue bonds could be paid promptly and in full. On the other hand, West Virginia refused to aid the defaulting West Virginia Turnpike and Chicago refused to aid the defaulting Calumet Skyway.

CHART 15
Proportionate Dollar Amounts Approved in State and Local Bond Elections and Debt Approved as a Percentage of Total Dollar Amount Subject to Election

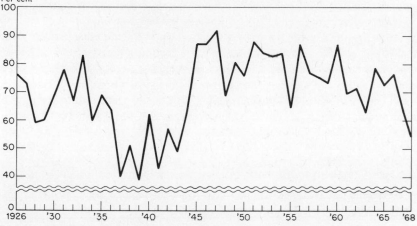

Debt Approved as Percentage of Total Dollar Amount Subject to Election

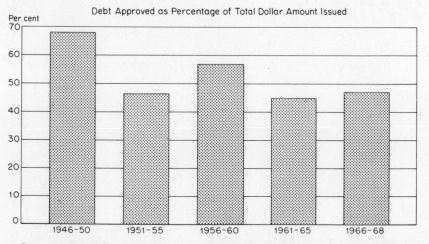

Debt Approved as Percentage of Total Dollar Amount Issued

Sources: The Bond Buyer, *Municipal Financial Statistics,* Vol. VII (April 1969); and the Investment Bankers Association, *Statistical Bulletins.*

The retirement arrangements for state and local debt is the second important measure indicating financial prudence and willingness to pay. Unmanageable debt service charges (often temporary) have been a cause of past difficulties. Two opposite extremes in debt retirement arrangements seem to have led
to payment difficulties. A kind of perennial optimism leads some state and
local borrowers to undertake loans for short periods, repayable in one or a
few very large instalments. If the maturity of these large instalments coincides
with an economic decline, financial difficulty is often the result. The oppos-
ing tendency is to stretch out the repayment period over too long a time
interval. Such a debt retirement arrangement risks decay or obsolescence of
the improvement before the last of the debt has been repaid.

State and local units generally seem to have been exercising prudent debt
retirement practices throughout the postwar period. Chart 10 (page 61) demonstrated that the maturity schedules had not shifted much in the late 1950's
and the early mid-1960's. Throughout the postwar period most state and
local debt was scheduled to mature within the probable useful life of the
improvement. Nearly all general obligations are now serial bonds with reason-

CHART 16

Median Proportion of Property Taxes Uncollected in Year
Assessed for Approximately 200 Largest U.S. Cities, 1928-67

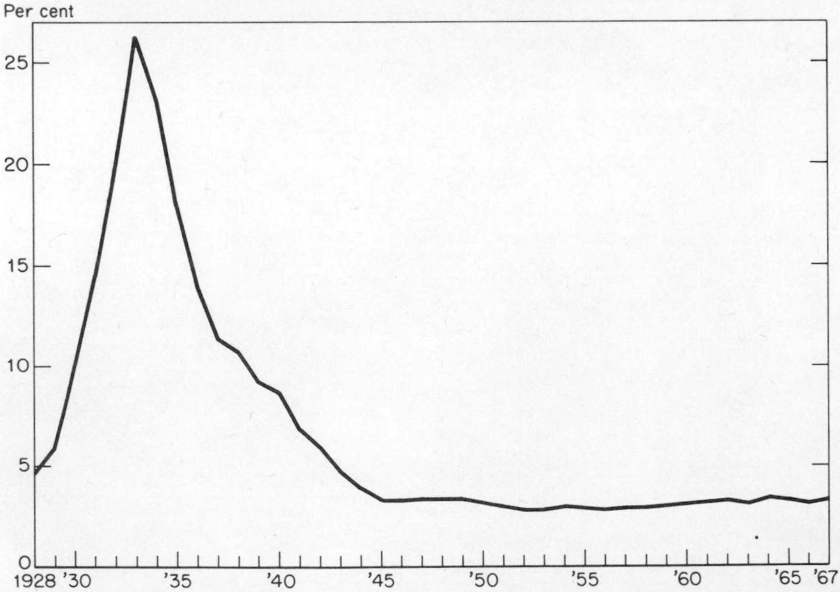

Note: Data from 1928-46 for cities with populations of over 50,000 in 1940; this
totaled 197 cities. After 1946 data was for the 200 largest cities.

Sources: Medians for 1928 and 1929 were computed from Dun & Bradstreet data by
the NBER staff. Remaining figures are from unpublished Dun & Bradstreet data.

ably level debt service payments scheduled throughout the life of the bond. The use of serial general obligations generally contributes to effective financial systems; however, serial maturities inject greater rigidity into budget charges for debt service in times of stress. A sizable number of limited liability obligations have term maturities; however, many of these bonds have sinking funds for debt retirement. The primary negative aspect in current debt retirement arrangements seems to be a disregard of obsolescence in estimating the probable useful life of some improvements. Chart 5 shows that over 45 per cent of state and local debt outstanding in 1962 matured in over twelve and one-half years. It appears that some improvements, e.g., toll road revenue bonds maturing in thirty or forty years, may be technologically obsolete before the bonds which finance them mature.

Another type of variable which may aid in assessing financial prudence and willingness to pay is the proportionate amount of state and local debt approved in bond elections. The top portion of Chart 15 traces the amount of indebtedness approved as a percentage of the total amount subject to state and local bond elections from 1926 through 1968. There has been a slight downward trend in the percentage approved in the postwar years; however, the average percentage approved in the 1960's is approximately the same as the percentage approved in the 1920's and early 1930's.

The bottom portion of Chart 15 compares the dollar amount approved in bond elections over five year periods with the amount of debt issued in the same five year periods. The 1966 − 68 period covers the latest three years for which data are available. The amount approved relative to the amount issued has been lower in the 1960's than in the late 1940's or 1950's. This finding should probably have been anticipated by the larger proportion of limited liability obligations and special district and statutory authority debt in the 1960's. The fact that a smaller portion of debt issued is approved by the electorate of the issuing body − whether because less is subject to electoral approval or because less is approved in such elections − would appear to weaken financial prudence and willingness to pay.

The last type of variable which may be indicative of financial prudence and willingness to pay is the measurement of the revenue collection performance of state and local governmental units. At the present time there is only one available measure which aids in evaluating the revenue collection performance. This measure is the proportion of current property taxes currently delinquent for the 200 largest cities. The median per cent of current property taxes which were delinquent for these units between 1928 and 1967 are revealed in Chart 16. The information in this chart shows that, while the proportion of currently delinquent property taxes has risen slightly in recent years, delinquent property taxes are proportionately much less than they were thoughout the 1930's. The reassuring implication of this analysis must be tempered by the fact that tax delinquencies have coincided in time with past defaults rather than leading them and by the wide dispersion among tax delinquencies. For example, in 1967, roughly 8 per cent of the largest cities had current tax delinquencies of over 10 per cent.[17]

Evaluation of Effects of Aggregate Characteristics

The following interpretations represent the author's evaluation of the postwar level of and changes in aggregate instrument and borrower characteristics. In the author's evaluation, the combined aggregate instrument and borrower characteristics affecting the quality of state and local debt, taken alone, indicate that the over-all quality of state and local debt has weakened in the postwar period. This conclusion of weakened quality is based on the assumption that the external environment has not changed appreciably. The starting or absolute level of quality of state and local debt in the immediate postwar period is not judged at this point.

State and local debt, and the resulting debt service charges, increased very rapidly throughout the postwar period. Cash resources which can be used to pay state and local debt service charges appear to have grown less rapidly than debt service charges. Postwar trends in the three areas determining cash resources lend support to this conclusion. First, over-all state and local cash inflows grew nearly as rapidly as debt service charges. The tax base and tax-paying ability, on which these cash inflows depend and which must ultimately come from the wealth, production and income of the U. S. economy, however, grew much less rapidly than debt service charges. Also, a larger proportion of postwar state and local cash inflows come from taxes based on cyclically vulnerable income and consumption.

Second, the proportion of state and local cash inflows which can be used to meet debt service charges appears to have fallen in the postwar period. This relative decline was caused by the higher degree of restricted use of state and local revenues and by the greater degree of rigidity in many state and local expenditures that must be paid prior to meeting debt service charges. Third, the stock of money and other liquid assets that state and local units have which might be available to meet debt service charges has not grown as fast as debt service charges in the postwar period.

Financial prudence and willingness to pay on the part of the issuing unit presents a heterogenous picture in the postwar period. The organization, quality of personnnel and techniques used in state and local financial administration appear to have improved in the postwar period. Most postwar borrowing has been for capital improvements and, in the aggregate, state and local units have not had deficits in their current accounts. Also, debt retirement arrangements do not seem to have changed appreciably in the postwar period.

---

[17]Based on unpublished information from Dun and Bradstreet. Unfortunately, dispersions were not readily available for other years.

Factors which may weaken financial prudence and willingness to pay include: (1) the increased state and local borrowing for essentially private purposes; (2) the increased use of debt payable solely from certain designated revenues; (3) the increased borrowing by special districts and statutory authorities (often not requiring voter approval, not subject to debt restrictions and concealed from many voters and taxpayers); and (4) the fact that some state and local improvements may be technologically obsolete before the bonds financing them mature.

Appendix:
The Identification of Quantitative Characteristics
Associated with Defaults on Municipal General Obligations[18]

The Sample Tested

In order to use multivariate statistical techniques it was necessary to find a sample of municipal general obligations in which a fairly large number of defaults had occurred. The most recent period which fulfilled these conditions was the early 1930's. Unfortunately, there was only one source of accurate default data and adequate quantitative characteristics which might determine the payment performance of general obligations in this period: the quantitative information on Michigan municipalities maintained at the Municipal Advisory Council of Michigan. The late Louis H. Schimmel, past president of the Council, allowed us to use this data to test the effect of the available quantitative characteristics on payment performance.

Use of this quantitative information on general obligations of Michigan municipalities in the 1930's introduced several possible sources of bias. The results of the statistical tests used may be representative for one geographic area (and not of the rest of the United States) and for one time period (which might have had different causes of payment problems than other periods). Also, the quantitative information available at the present time is greater and is more detailed than that available for Michigan municipalities in the 1930's. This was, however, the only known sample where there was both an adequate amount of defaults, by far the preferable measure of debt payment performance, and an adequate amount of quantitative information.

The sample selected for analysis in this paper was twenty-four of the twenty-five largest cities in Michigan in the 1930's. Initial tests and a case history of the Detroit situation suggested that it was a special case which should be excluded from the sample. Seventeen of the twenty-four Michigan cities studied had some debts in default during the 1929-37 period. At the end of 1933, when all of these seventeen units were in default and when the amount in default was the highest, $4,878,000 of the $102,612,000 of total debt outstanding for the twenty-four units was in direct default.

[18]This appendix consists of exerpts from a more comprehensive study financed by the Relm Foundation of Ann Arbor, Michigan.

The eleven available quantitative characteristics for this sample that might affect the payment performance of these Michigan municipal units were:

X_1 — dollar amount of notes outstanding
X_2 — population
X_3 — total assessed property values
X_4 — dollar amount of taxes levied
X_5 — tax levy per $1,000 assessed value
X_6 — dollar amount of debt outstanding
X_7 — per capita debt
X_8 — debt/assessed property values
X_9 — per cent of current taxes delinquent
X_{10} — tax levy per capita
X_{11} — assessed property values per capita

The population figures were from the 1930 census, the assessed values were for the 1932-33 fiscal year, while the remaining measures were as of July 1933.

Three multivariable statistical techniques — factor analysis, multiple discriminate analysis and multiple regression — were used to examine the relationship between these quantitative measures and the payment records of the twenty-four units studied. Factor analysis was used to try to identify groupings of measures affecting the dollar amount in default. Several different high vs. low default classes were used with multiple discriminate analysis. The discriminate function between the seven cities with no defaults on their indebtedness and the seventeen cities with one or more defaulted issues seemed most meaningful on conceptual grounds and provided the most meaningful results. The proportionate amount of outstanding indebtedness in default at the end of 1933 was used on the dependent variable in the regression analysis.

Results of Factor Analysis

Factor analysis identified four potential groupings of the quantitative characteristics. These groupings, with a descriptive title selected by the author, and their characteristics are listed in the order of their relevance to the group.

Aggregate Size Characteristics
X_2 — population
X_4 — dollar amount of taxes levied
X_3 — total assessed property value
X_6 — dollar amount of debt outstanding
X_1 — dollar amount of notes outstanding
Relative Tax and Debt Burden

X_8 — debt/assessed property values
X_9 — per cent of current taxes delinquent
X_7 — per capita debt
X_5 — tax levy per $1,000 assessed property values
Per Capita Wealth, Taxes and Debt
X_{11} — assessed property values per capita
X_{10} — tax levy per capita
X_7 — per capita debt
Willingness to Pay Characteristics
X_9 — per cent of current taxes delinquent
X_{10} — tax levy per capita
X_5 — tax levy per $1,000 assessed property values
X_1 — dollar amount of notes outstanding

The willingness to pay characteristics had an eigen value considerably below the generally acceptable level of 2.0. The three other factor groupings explained slightly over 80 per cent of the variance in the proportionate dollar amounts in default of the twenty-four units.

Results of Multiple Discriminate Analysis
Initially all eleven available quantitative characteristics were used to discriminate between the seventeen municipal units which defaulted and seven units which did not default during the period. Four characteristics — tax rate per $1,000 of assessed valuation (X_5), per capita debt (X_7), debt assessed property values (X_8) and the tax delinquency rate (X_9) — were significant at the $p < .10$ level (using the t test). The probability that the discriminate function was due to chance was a relatively high .22. The confusion matrix (assuming equal a priori probabilities and equal costs), however, showed only one misclassification between the nondefaulting and defaulting groups.

Various numbers and combinations of the available characteristics were then tried to improve the discriminate function. The most impressive results occurred when four characteristics — tax rate per $1,000 assessed valuation (X_5), per capita debt (X_7), tax delinquency rate (X_9) and assessed property values per capita (X_{11}) — were used. None of the characteristics was almost a linear combination of the other characteristics, three of the four characteristics were significant at the $p < .10$ level (using the t test), and the probability that the discriminate function was due to chance fell to .04. The confusion matrix however (assuming equal a priori probabilities and equal cost) indicated there were three misclassifications between the defaulting and nondefaulting groups. The results were very similar when debt/assessed property values (X_8) was substituted for per capita debt (X_7).

Discriminate analysis was also tried with several other high vs. low default classes, e. g., municipal units with less than 5 per cent of their outstanding indebtedness in default vs. those with over 5 per cent of their debt in default. The significant characteristics were generally the same; however, as the classifying proportionate amount in default increased, the dollar amount of notes outstanding (X_1) and the tax levy per capita (X_{10}) tended to become more significant (usually at the $p < .10$ level) and per capita debt (X_7) became less significant. The probability that the discriminate function was due to chance was usually higher and there were more misclassifications in the confusion matrix with these classes than with the default vs. nondefault classes.

Results of Regression Analysis

Multiple linear regression analysis using the proportionate amount of outstanding indebtedness in default as the dependent variable (y) identified similar quantitative characteristics as being related to debt payment performance. The following multiple linear regression equation resulted when the regression coefficients that were not significant at the $p < .10$ level (using the t test) were eliminated:

$$y = -.1888 - \underset{(.0000018)}{.0000049X_2} + \underset{(.00000009)}{.00000026X_4} + \underset{(.00625)}{.00929X_5}$$

$$\underset{(.00153)}{-.00347X_7} + \underset{(1.262)}{3.1999X_8} + \underset{(.080)}{.194X_9} - \underset{(.0061)}{.0163X_{10}} + \underset{(.000127)}{.000305X_{11}}$$

The quantitative characteristics in this regression equation explained approximately 64 per cent of the observed differences in the municipalities default ratios. All of the regression coefficients were significant at the $p < .025$ level (using the t test), with the exception of the coefficient of X_5 which was significant at the $p < .075$ level. While the variables in a regression equation should primarily be looked at as acting together, it was worrisome that the multicollinearity between some of the independent variables caused the coefficients of several of these variables to have signs the opposite of those predicted by the conceptual model.

When the multicollinearity is restricted, the coefficients of the independent variables, quantitative characteristics, have signs consistent with the conceptual model. Multicollinearity is restricted when at least one of the size characteristics, X_2 or X_4, is eliminated; when only one of the debt burden measures, X_7 or X_8, is used; and when either tax levy per capita, X_{10}, or assessed property values per capita, X_{11}, is eliminated. Since the t value of either X_2 or X_4 fails drastically if one of these two size characteristics is eliminated, it seems appropriate to eliminate both of these variables. The following multiple coefficients of determination result from the following combination of variables:

$$r^2 = .44 \qquad r^2 = .43 \qquad r^2 = .42 \qquad r^2 = .40$$

X_5	X_5	X_5	X_5
X_8	X_8	X_7	X_7
X_9	X_9	X_9	X_9
X_{10}	X_{11}	X_{10}	X_{11}

The multiple linear regression equation with the highest r^2 was:

$$y = .06142 - .00310X_5 + .3521X_8 + .07209X_9 - .00115X_{10}$$
$$\quad\quad\quad (.00247) \quad\quad (.1700) \quad\quad (.07277) \quad\quad (.00108)$$

All of the variables in this and the other three equations were significant at the $p < .10$ level and the signs of the coefficients could always be explained in terms of the conceptual model.

When multicollinearity is restricted, the signs of the variables in both the discriminate analysis and the regression analysis seem consistent with the conceptual model formulated in Chapter 2 of this study. Debt to assessed property values, or per capita debt, would seem to be a meaningful proxy for the relationship between debt service charges and revenues available to meet those charges. Assessed property values per capita and the property tax levy per \$1,000 of assessed property values should indicate the relative wealth of the unit and the extent to which the municipal government is tapping this wealth. These characteristics should improve the quality of the debt to assessed property value or population ratio. The tax levy per capita and tax delinquency rate would seem to fit into the conceptual model as tests of the financial prudence and willingness to pay of the municipal government and its constituents.

Conclusions

Multivariable statistical techniques indicated that the quantitative characteristics of the twenty-four Michigan municipalities were good indicators of payment performance in the 1930's. Nearly all of the quantitative characteristics seemed significant except for the size characteristics — population, amount of notes, amount of long-term debt, total assessed property values and amount of taxes levied. This exception was probably at least partially caused by the sample selected — the second through the twenty-fifth largest cities in Michigan.

6

CHARACTERISTICS OF SELECTED CLASSIFICATIONS OF STATE AND LOCAL DEBT

Up to this point, it has been implied that state and local debt consists of a group of reasonably similar debt instruments. Individual instruments, however, often differ substantially on important characteristics such as the type of issuer, the legal liability and the type of resources pledged for debt service payments. There may be sizeable differences in quality among different classifications of state and local debt. The possibility exists, therefore, that changes in the composition of state and local debt have affected the quality of such debt.

The proportionate amounts of the three major classifications of state and local debt and some of the characteristics that may indicate quality within these classifications are presented in this chapter. Discussion of the first two methods of classification, by type of governmental unit and by geographic region, is brief due to the lack of detailed data and because the differences in quality do not appear to have a very large impact on the quality of state and local debt. The third method of classification, by type of resources used to pay debt service charges, is discussed more thoroughly because of large shifts in the proportionate amount of state and local debt classified in this matter and because of their possible relevance to the over-all quality of state and local debt.

Classification by Type of Governmental Unit

The types of state and local units issuing debt include:
  States
  Regular local governmental units
    Counties and parishes

Incorporated municipalities (cities, towns, etc.)
Unincorporated municipalities (townships, etc.)

Special districts
School districts
Drainage, irrigation, levee districts
Sewer and water districts
Road, bridge, and street districts
Miscellaneous (fire, park, etc.) districts

Statutory authorities
Port authorities
Bridge authorities
Housing authorities
Toll road commissions
Miscellaneous (power, canal, dormitory, parking, school,
airport, etc.) authorities

This method of classification points out some of the differences among state and local governmental units. State governments, with the exception of New York, are the only government units below the federal level which may not be sued by individuals or corporations without the consent of the involved unit. State and regular local governments, such as counties and cities, possess broad powers such as the police power, the taxation power and the power of eminent domain. The activities of states and regular local governments generally produce no revenue and taxes are their principal sources of income. State and regular local governments ordinarily issue debt by pledging their credit; however, they may pledge specific revenues or create a special district or authority to issue bonds. Special districts are similar to regular governmental units in their power to tax, but they are usually organized to promote a specific activity. Statutory authorities are public corporations, without the power to tax, which generally operate revenue-producing projects.

The amount of debt outstanding for each of the major types of state and local units from 1902 through 1968 is presented in Appendix Table 3. The borrower characteristics for the major types of state and local units in 1952 and 1966 are presented in Table 14. Analysis of these data reveals that debt service charges were a rising percentage of the general revenues for all types of state and local units between 1952 and 1966. In both of these years the debt service charges for incorporated municipalities and special districts were a much higher proportion of their general revenues than the similar relationship for the other major state and local units. Between 1952 and 1966 the growth in debt service charges as a per cent of general revenues was by far the greatest for special districts — debt service charges increased over six times while general revenues increased less than four times.

TABLE 14

Debt and Borrower Characteristics, Classified by Type of Governmental Unit
(dollar figures in millions)

	All State & Local Units	State[a]	Counties & Parishes	Incorporated Municipalities	Unincorporated Municipalities	School Districts	Special Districts[a]
1952							
Debt outstanding	30,100	6,874	2,018	12,659	619	3,806	4,125
Interest charges	724	144	49	341	15	94	81
Est. debt service charges[b]	2,367	587	204	980	54	315	228
General revenues[c]	25,181	13,529	3,926	6,351	833	5,087	669
Revenues from own sources[d]	22,615	10,944	2,385	5,139	594	2,920	632
Property taxes	8,652	370	1,835	3,144	515	2,618	170
General expenditures[e]	26,098	13,697	4,015	6,303	993	5,342	1,236
Interest/general revenues	2.5%	1.1%	1.2%	5.4%	1.8%	1.8%	12.1%
DSCs/general revenues	9.4%	4.3%	5.2%	15.4%	6.5%	6.2%	34.1%
Interest/own revenues	2.8%	1.3%	2.1%	6.6%	2.5%	3.2%	12.8%
DSCs/own revenues	10.5%	5.4%	8.6%	19.1%	9.1%	10.8%	36.1%
1966							
Debt outstanding	107,051	29,564	7,208	33,714	1,989	17,841	16,736
Interest charges	3,268	894	234	1,013	54	561	512
Est. debt service charges[b]	8,688	2,112	621	2,936	172	1,527	1,320
General revenues[c]	83,036	46,757	11,444	17,262	2,109	20,946	2,509
Revenue from own sources[d]	69,916	34,511	6,829	13,122	1,610	11,886	1,959
Property taxes	24,670	834	4,939	6,879	1,340	10,102	576
General expenditures[e]	82,842	46,010	10,774	17,047	2,026	21,176	2,658
Interest/general revenues	3.9%	1.9%	2.0%	5.9%	2.6%	2.2%	20.4%
DSCs/general revenues	10.5%	4.5%	5.4%	17.0%	8.2%	7.3%	52.6%
Interest/own revenues	4.7%	2.6%	3.4%	7.7%	3.3%	4.7%	26.1%
DSCs/own revenues	12.4%	6.1%	9.1%	22.4%	10.7%	12.8%	67.4%

Notes to Table 14

Sources: U.S. Department of Commerce, *Historical Statistics on Governmental Finances,* Vol. VI, No. 4 of *1962 Census of Governments; Governmental Finances in 1954;* and *Governmental Finances in 1965-66.*

[a]Statutory authorities are included primarily in the states and special districts categories.

[b]Estimated debt service charges include interest charges and long-term debt redeemed but not refunded and does not include short-term debt.

[c]General revenues exclude utility revenues, liquor revenues and insurance trust revenues. General revenues include intergovernmental revenues so the sum for the individual types of governmental units does not equal the total for all units.

[d]General revenues excluding all intergovernmental revenues.

[e]General expenditures exclude utility expenditures, liquor store expenditures and insurance trust expenditures. General expenditures include intergovernmental grants so the sum of expenditures for individual types of governmental units does not equal the total for all state and local units.

While classification as to type of unit may be useful in describing some of the differences among state and local indebtedness, this method has several major disadvantages when assessing the quality of state and local debt. First, economic and intangible factors generally outweigh the legal features stressed in classification by type of unit. For example, neither the legal-inability-to-sue feature of state bonds nor the limited powers of school districts appear to detract substantially from the investment appeal, *ceteris paribus,* of these classes of state and local debt. Second, it is not possible to classify the resources on which government revenues are based by type of state or local unit. For example, wealth and income measures cannot be separated by type of government unit. Third, other useful data, such as the size of the tax base and the liquid asset balances, are not compiled by type of state and local unit at the present time. Finally, there are conceptual problems, such as the interpretation of intergovernmental revenues and expenditures and the lack of separate data for statutory authorities, which complicate the analysis of what data are available.

Classification by Geographic Region

An alternative method of classifying state and local debt is by geographic region. The earlier data on payment difficulties indicate the potential importance of such information. For example, prior to the 1929 major default period several areas, e.g., Florida and the Far West, experienced rapid growth in indebtedness with little realized growth in resources, to repay such indebtedness. These areas experienced serious defaults when the expected growth in

TABLE 15

State and Local Debt in Relation to Revenue, Income and Wealth Measures,
by States in 1942, 1957 and 1966

		1942		
	Debt/Pop.	Debt/ Personal Income	Debt/ General Revenues	Debt/ Own Revenues
Alabama	$ 74.18	.143	2.052	2.320
Alaska	n.a.	n.a.	n.a.	n.a.
Arizona	143.66	.158	1.579	1.864
Arkansas	114.58	.243	3.066	3.461
California	172.47	.133	1.602	1.746
Colorado	137.54	.152	1.380	1.613
Connecticut	105.15	.074	1.154	1.230
Delaware	95.73	.075	1.384	1.549
Dist. of Columbia	24.54	.018	.349	.413
Florida	209.30	.270	3.020	3.304
Georgia	44.21	.077	1.102	1.226
Hawaii	n.a.	n.a.	n.a.	n.a.
Idaho	159.60	.175	1.801	2.115
Illinois	118.95	.115	1.420	1.525
Indiana	48.47	.053	.697	.766
Iowa	69.39	.084	.887	.961
Kansas	59.42	.070	.807	.905
Kentucky	50.24	.094	1.167	1.312
Louisiana	151.55	.256	2.411	2.659
Maine	83.76	.099	1.171	1.295
Maryland	162.54	.144	2.508	2.687
Massachusetts	122.58	.114	1.293	1.390
Michigan	113.48	.108	1.369	1.474
Minnesota	117.86	.148	1.224	1.346
Mississippi	82.34	.188	1.934	2.221
Missouri	84.46	.104	1.390	1.579
Montana	173.87	.193	1.689	1.929
Nebraska	159.51	.196	2.302	2.610
Nevada	75.79	.048	.585	.789
New Hampshire	71.74	.084	.823	.908

repayment sources failed to materialize or the economy declined. Such payment difficulties obviously affected the involved geographic region and may also have contributed to problems in other areas by changing the willingness to pay of some governmental units and the public's willingness to lend to state and local units.

Using such a method of classification involves several problems. What geographic region should be used — political divisions, economic regions or metropolitan areas? There is the problem of finding the debt service charges

	1957				1966		
Debt/Pop.	Debt/ Personal Income	Debt/ General Revenues	Debt/ Own Revenues	Debt/Pop.	Debt/ Personal Income	Debt/ General Revenues	Debt/ Own Revenues
$200.53	.148	1.219	1.522	$444.40	.215	1.309	1.808
191.32	.082	.916	1.212	959.29	.280	1.141	2.052
270.19	.152	1.156	1.326	467.20	.184	1.009	1.266
167.16	.141	1.079	1.329	287.34	.143	.893	1.231
321.08	.129	1.047	1.173	661.25	.191	1.160	1.388
286.99	.142	1.058	1.241	492.85	.169	.948	1.176
474.25	.173	2.011	2.128	792.27	.215	1.867	2.136
516.92	.181	2.455	2.700	1213.87	.344	2.341	2.751
111.60	.041	.437	.533	402.06	.108	.794	1.086
287.28	.162	1.360	1.511	516.27	.198	1.345	1.567
232.24	.161	1.226	1.506	408.27	.172	1.197	1.507
376.01	.200	1.523	1.784	744.27	.238	1.300	1.632
148.63	.089	.649	.771	251.73	.103	.565	.704
324.19	.131	1.489	1.600	487.23	.138	1.215	1.387
176.86	.087	.968	1.039	312.61	.102	.782	.886
118.61	.063	.508	.563	208.37	.070	.461	.538
306.02	.170	1.318	1.493	448.67	.157	1.031	1.212
157.39	.110	1.005	1.175	534.70	.238	1.622	2.139
356.60	.237	1.397	1.639	581.68	.255	1.361	1.738
205.83	.122	1.063	1.209	307.83	.124	.838	1.040
503.52	.227	2.404	2.625	654.43	.204	1.637	1.870
437.84	.190	1.771	1.909	634.14	.194	1.426	1.651
243.42	.109	1,018	1.106	499.18	.153	1.122	1.285
217.32	.115	.877	.972	503.76	.174	1.011	1.205
153.68	.152	.927	1.117	370.62	.209	1.154	1.514
166.43	.084	.907	1.087	340.83	.121	.911	1.140
217.59	.113	.784	.953	356.73	.136	.721	.957
358.73	.190	1.786	2.031	533.70	.184	1.391	1.661
253.31	.102	.701	.848	595.03	.170	1.035	1.331
213.75	.114	1.089	1.200	407.86	.145	1.183	1.418

(continued)

and resources available to pay debt service charge measures or proxies for such measures for the types of regions selected. Finally, what is to be done with overlapping debt, i.e., debt in two or more of the regions selected?

Table 15 is an example of what can be done with state and local debt classified by geographic regions. Statewide regions were selected, and the relationships examined were debt/population, debt/personal income, debt/general revenues and debt/general revenues from own sources. Debt is a proxy

TABLE 15 concluded

		1942		
	Debt/Pop.	Debt/ Personal Income	Debt/ General Revenues	Debt/ Own Revenues
New Jersey	$254.43	.217	2.771	2.893
New Mexico	128.32	.202	1.738	2.004
New York	399.45	.341	3.314	3.445
North Carolina	121.03	.209	2.422	2.636
North Dakota	72.21	.110	.665	.729
Ohio	99.18	.096	1.287	1.402
Oklahoma	79.78	.127	1.190	1.215
Oregon	139.56	.120	1.495	1.695
Pennsylvania	155.25	.165	1.941	2.117
Rhode Island	245.00	.209	3.266	3.494
South Carolina	103.50	.191	2.171	2.556
South Dakota	116.84	.155	1.233	1.391
Tennessee	131.32	.235	2.950	3.297
Texas	109.38	.152	2.080	2.302
Utah	72.07	.080	.828	1.002
Vermont	51.01	.067	.658	.737
Virginia	71.24	.084	1.495	1.638
Washington	123.27	.102	1.282	1.501
West Virginia	73.35	.120	1.258	1.420
Wisconsin	39.22	.045	.418	.449
Wyoming	203.98	.218	2.046	2.459
U.S. average	143.38	.157	1.856	2.023
Median state	113.48	.127	1.369	1.579

Sources: U.S. Department of Commerce, *Historical Statistics on Governmental Finances,* Vol. IV, No. 4 of *1962 Census of Governments,* and *Governmental Finances in 1965-66.*

n.a. = not available.

for debt service charges while the measures related to debt are proxies for the resources available to pay debt service charges. The information is presented for three years: 1942, 1957 and 1966.

The data in Table 15 indicate that the relationships between debt and the surrogates for resources that can be used to pay debt service charges varied greatly among statewide areas and were not consistent for broader sections of the country. Futhermore, these relationships changed rather markedly over time. During World War II, the eight states with the heaviest amount of state and local debt relative to the resource surrogates were Arkansas, Florida,

1957				1966			
Debt/Pop.	Debt/ Personal Income	Debt/ General Revenues	Debt/ Own Revenues	Debt/Pop.	Debt/ Personal Income	Debt/ General Revenues	Debt/ Own Revenues
$397.33	.160	1.879	1.971	$509.75	.148	1.332	1.487
237.39	.144	.834	1.076	382.94	.161	.709	1.007
596.63	.237	2.134	2.260	971.91	.278	1.840	2.013
186.31	.136	1.123	1.342	246.47	.108	.791	.961
138.49	.090	.507	.578	295.46	.124	.620	.757
281.68	.127	1.434	1.558	439.06	.144	1.228	1.438
246.29	.151	1.069	1.295	473.51	.192	1.123	1.468
268.37	.135	.950	1.104	484.73	.167	.968	1.246
320.78	.149	1.619	1.730	585.64	.197	1.622	1.882
320.79	.161	1.657	1.887	599.47	.197	1.497	1.830
187.21	.151	1.207	1.392	219.22	.107	.782	.963
68.75	.042	.275	.329	144.31	.060	.329	.419
282.01	.199	1.716	2.003	509.43	.229	1.612	2.088
324.92	.178	1.608	1.845	500.58	.197	1.444	1.735
200.29	.113	.861	1.008	460.27	.185	.986	1.307
149.93	.090	.673	.775	336.31	.130	.713	.974
205.62	.124	1.190	1.313	368.34	.141	1.115	1.379
493.87	.231	1.858	2.093	1215.10	.377	2.315	2.773
215.01	.129	1.338	1.533	339.37	.156	.947	1.298
156.40	.079	.673	.725	417.38	.140	.922	1.029
211.30	.102	.613	.817	422.45	.154	.628	.992
311.31	.152	1.390	1.545	546.57	.185	1.289	1.531
237.39	.136	1.089	1.313	467.20	.169	1.122	1.379

Louisiana, New Jersey, New York, Rhode Island, Tennessee and Wyoming. By 1957, the eight states with the heaviest amount of state and local debt were Connecticut, Delaware, Louisiana, Maryland, Massachusetts, Nebraska, New York and Washington. By 1966, the eight states with the heaviest debt burden were Alaska, Connecticut, Delaware, Kentucky, Maryland, New York, Tennessee and Washington.[1]

Many other instrument and borrower characteristics should be considered before reaching a conclusion about the quality of state and local debt by statewide areas. Analysis of quality by geographic regions (e.g., Table 15 plus additional available characteristics) is a useful tool in spotting areas of potential debt payment difficulties. Such analysis must be used with greater cau-

[1]The states with the heaviest debt burden were selected by ranking the four debt to resources ratios in declining order and arithmetically weighting these ratios from 1 to 50. The eight states with the lowest combined weights are listed for each period.

tion when assessing the quality of all state and local debt in the United States. If only a few geographic regions had debt payment difficulties it seems reasonable that shifts in intergovernmental revenues might help alleviate the difficulties until correcting adjustments could be made.

Classification by Type of Resources Used to Pay Debt Service Charges

A third method of classifying state and local debt is by the type of resources used to pay debt service charges. Numerous categories can be formed using this basis of classification. However, by reevaluating several relatively small classifications of state and local debt, four major categories, which encompass nearly all state and local debt, can be distinguished. The relative dollar amount of state and local debt outstanding in each of these categories — guaranteed debt, short-term debt, limited liability obligation bonds and general obligation bonds — is illustrated in Chart 17. The quality of each of these major categories is briefly examined in the following paragraphs.

Guaranteed Debt

The first major category is housing authority notes and bonds issued under the provisions of the Federal Housing Act of 1949. While each such issue is secured by a pledge of the net rental revenues of the local project, it has additional strength based on the contribution contract with the Public Housing Authority. Since the Public Housing Authority unconditionally agrees to make annual contribution that would be sufficient to pay note and bond principal and interest when due, the faith and credit of an agency of the United States lies behind housing authority indebtedness. The dollar amount of housing authority notes and bonds issued annually is disclosed in Appendix Table 1 and the dollar amount outstanding appears in Appendix Table 2.[2] The relative dollar amount outstanding, illustrated graphically in Chart 17, has remained close to 5 per cent of all outstanding state and local debt since the early 1950's.

The quality of these Public Housing Authority notes and bonds is as good as the quality of an issue by a federal government agency. While the quality of this 5 per cent of state and local debt is very high, it does not mean its service charges should be ignored or that this category of indebtedness should be treated as federal rather than state or local. The debt service charges on Public Housing Authority notes and bonds are paid from the rental revenues

---

[2]Some notes and bonds were issued under the previous Housing Authority Act of 1939. The issues under the 1939 Act that were outstanding in 1949 were covered by the 1949 Act.

CHART 17

Proportionate Dollar Amount of State and Local Debt Outstanding, by Type of
Resources Used for Payments, 1902-68

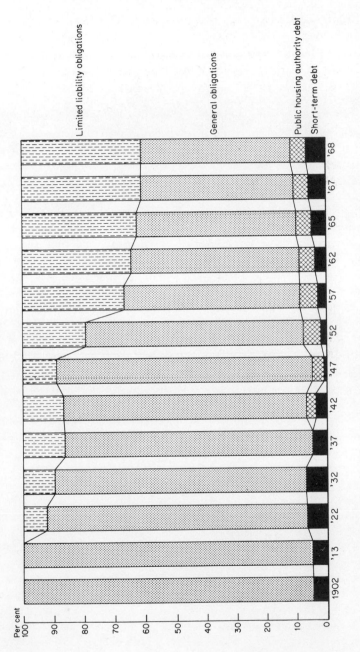

Note: General obligations include all debt other than short-term for 1902 and 1913.
Source: Data in Appendix Table 2.

of the housing projects (plus the ability to borrow to repay some of the notes), which are classified as general revenues of state and local units. Some revenues which are classified as state and local general revenues are, therefore, restricted to this purpose. The Public Housing Authority has been forced to contribute to debt service charges in only a few instances and their contribution typically have been only for short periods of time.

Short-Term Debt

The second major category is debt having a maturity of less than a year at issuance. Short-term Public Housing Authority notes are treated as guaranteed debt and not included in this category. Chart 17 shows that short-term debt was roughly 5 per cent of all state and local debt outstanding in 1902 and 1913. Short-term debt rose during the 1920's and early 1930's, reaching nearly 7 per cent of the total state and local debt outstanding by 1932. Short-term debt fell to less than 1 per cent of total state and local debt outstanding in the years immediately following World War II, then increased steadily, reaching approximately 5 per cent of debt outstanding by the end of 1968.

The major portion of short-term debt is tax anticipation notes, which are secured by tax receipts anticipated in the near future and by the full faith and credit of the issuing unit. Most of the remaining short-term debt is secured by both the proceeds of another planned debt issue and by the full faith and credit of the issuing state and local unit. Nearly all of the remainder of this category of state and local debt is secured by the full faith and credit of the issuing unit.

The resources that can be used to pay the debt service charges on short-term debt are, therefore, similar to those available for general obligation bonds. Because repayment of principal is always eminent, the liquid assets and borrowing reserve of the issuing unit assume a more prominent role. The borrowing reserve is probably best estimated by an analysis of the general quality of the issuing unit and its payment performance. Many units defaulted on short-term issues in the early 1930's because they were no longer able to borrow at any reasonable cost.

The relationship between short-term debt outstanding and liquid assets (currency and deposits in financial institutions) of state and local units from 1945 through 1968 appears in Chart 18. The data in Chart 18 show that short-term debt has become a larger and larger per cent of state and local liquid assets since the end of World War II. The growth in the early postwar years started from a very low base. The proportion of short-term debt, however, has continued to rise in the 1960's. This proportion has averaged close to 25 per cent in the mid-1960's. While exactly comparable figures are not available prior to 1945 it appears that short-term debt fluctuated between 20 and 30 per cent of state and local liquid assets in the 1920's and 1930's, and climbed to over 60 per cent of state and local liquid assets during the 1929-33

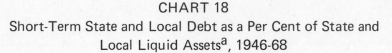

CHART 18
Short-Term State and Local Debt as a Per Cent of State and
Local Liquid Assets[a], 1946-68

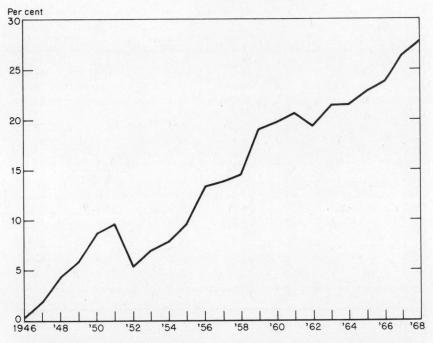

Sources: Short-term debt outstanding from Appendix Table 2. Liquid asset figures from Goldsmith, Lipsey and Mendelson, *Studies in the National Balance Sheet of the United States,* Vol. II, Table III-6, pp. 216-217; unpublished FRB worksheets; and *Governmental Finances,* 1959-68 issues.

depression period.

Limited Liability Obligation

Limited liability obligation bonds form the third category of state and local debt. Nearly all of the debt included in this category come under the conventional term "revenue bonds" or the Bureau of the Census term "non-guaranteed debt." The dollar amount of outstanding limited liability obligation bonds grew rapidly relative to other bonds, as can be seen in Charts 10 (page 61) and 17 (page 91). The data in Table 16, which shows the proportion of nonguaranteed debt by type of governmental unit, reinforce this rapid growth.

Limited liability bonds, which are long-term debts, are payable solely from the revenues derived from the operation of (1) the facilities constructed or acquired with the proceeds of the bonds or (2) other facilities owned by the

TABLE 16

Percentage of Long-Term Debt Outstanding Which Is Nonguaranteed,
by Type of Governmental Unit, 1948-68

Year	All State and Local	States	All Local[a]	Counties	Incorporated Municipalities	Unincorporated Municipalities	Special Districts[b]
1968	42.3	55.8	36.5	18.5	40.6	6.0	79.5
1967	41.7	56.5	35.6	14.2	39.0	4.4	81.4
1966	40.8	55.4	35.0	10.7	38.4	6.3	81.1
1965	40.1	55.0	34.4	11.8	36.9	6.2	81.8
1964	39.1	54.3	33.3	7.9	36.7	3.4	81.5
1963	39.0	53.2	33.7	10.5	36.2	4.7	83.2
1962	37.7	52.2	32.1	8.4	34.5	6.2	82.3
1961	37.6	51.2	32.4	10.8	34.8	4.3	82.1
1960	37.7	50.8	32.7	18.4	33.8	3.4	84.4
1959	35.8	50.0	30.5	13.0	34.0	5.2	84.3
1958	35.7	51.2	29.9	12.2	33.0	10.0	82.3
1957	35.3	52.0	29.2	16.0	31.7	15.9	79.5
1956	31.8	50.9	24.8	13.5	28.8	17.2	58.5
1955	30.6	45.9	25.3	12.2	29.0	28.8	57.9
1954	26.8	38.1	23.1	10.2	25.0	3.1	58.1
1953	24.2	31.3	19.7	12.2	23.8	5.7	43.6
1952	21.9	25.8	18.3	12.7	22.1	4.9	29.1
1951	16.4	22.1	14.6	3.1	20.6	1.4	16.2
1950	14.1	18.0	13.0	3.0	17.4	1.3	15.3
1949	12.3	15.4	11.5	2.7	12.0	.8	23.4
1948	10.6	10.6	10.6	2.7	10.4	.8	22.4

Sources: U.S. Department of Commerce, *Historical Statistics on Governmental Finances*, Vol. IV, No. 4 of *1962 Census of Governments;* and *Governmental Finances in 1963-68*, an annual publication.

[a]Includes school districts that are not listed separately because they had no nonguaranteed debt during the entire period covered.

[b]Other than school districts that are not listed separately because they had no nonguaranteed debt during the entire period covered.

issuer of the bonds. Long-term state and local issues that are payable from a limited or special tax or from specified rents, leases or appropriations are also classified as limited liability obligation bonds. The security for limited liability obligations is based primarily upon the specific revenue-producing activity, special tax or special fund, rather than primarily upon the economic resources of the taxpayers. This type of debt financing, therefore, opens sources of revenue that typically would not be available through general obligation financing.

A limited liability bond issued by a government unit is an obligation of that unit, but the unit's legal obligation only extends to the bond service payments from a specified source of revenue. This limited security was a cause of the relatively poorer payment performance of these obligations in the postwar period (documented in Chapter 3). There is considerable disagreement on whether an issuing or benefiting government unit has a "moral" obligation to implement its revenue bonds by providing financial assistance. During the postwar period, some issuing or benefiting units have aided their limited liability bonds, while others have openly refused to do so.[3] It appears inappropriate to assume that a possible moral obligation on the part of another public body will prove financially productive.

If it is accepted that limited liability obligations will be paid solely from the pledged source, debt service costs on these obligations can be compared directly with the cash flows pledged to cover the service charges.[4] Chart 19 compares the cash coverage of larger limited liability obligations for alternate years from 1955 through 1969. The data in Chart 19 demonstrates that the average cash flow coverage of all the limited liability obligations observed (constituting over 50 per cent of the dollar amount of all limited liabilities outstanding) has had a modest upward trend over the period observed. Much of this increase appears to be due to the sharply increased cash flow coverage of service charges on debts paid from tolls on roads or bridges.

The data in Table 17 show that the improved cash flow coverage of debt service charges does not extend to all limited liability obligations. As late as 1967 approximately 19 per cent of the limited liability obligations analyzed by Standard and Poor's covered debt service charges less than 1.25 times. Among toll road issues approximately 36 per cent covered debt service charges 1.25 times or less.

The improved cash flow coverage of limited liability debt service charges indicates the quality of this particular classification of debt has improved slightly in the last decade or so. The implications for the quality of all state and local debt are more complicated. Limited liability obligations made new sources of revenues available, often at the cost of lower security. The rapid increase in the relative amount of a generally weaker quality obligation (Table 16 shows limited liability obligations rose from approximately 10 per cent to approximately 40 per cent of the dollar amount of all long-term state and local debt outstanding during the postwar period) was probably at the expense of slower relative growth in the usually higher quality general obliga-

---

[3]For example, Kansas City, Missouri, advanced supplementary funds so that interest on its Auditorium Plaza Garage revenue bonds could be paid promptly and in full. On the other hand, West Virginia refused to aid the defaulting West Virginia Turnpike.

[4]There is generally no attempt to maximize these cash flows once they adequately cover debt service charges; therefore, the aggregative cash coverage of limited liability obligations is not maximized. Two possible methods of overcoming this problem — using the asset values of the facilities and estimating maximum cash flows — are not practical at this time due to the lack of adequate data.

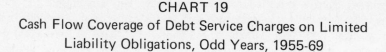

CHART 19
Cash Flow Coverage of Debt Service Charges on Limited Liability Obligations, Odd Years, 1955-69

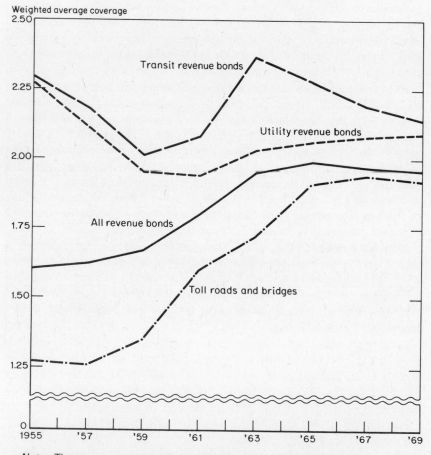

Note: The separate purpose categories do not add up to the total category.

Source: Standard and Poor's Corporation, *Municipal Bond Selectors.* The first issue of a year was used as the coverage for the preceding year.

tions. There is evidence that government units were forced to issue sizeable amounts of limited liability obligations because of outmoded restrictions limiting general obligation debt.[5] It would appear that the shift in composition toward a higher portion of indebtedness of a weaker quality, other things being equal, has had a weakening effect on the over-all quality of state and local debt. Furthermore, since revenues pledged to cover limited liability

[5]For example, see James A. Heins, *Constitutional Restrictions Against State Debt,* Madison, Wis. 1963.

obligations are usually restricted to this purpose, the growth in revenues from such obligations will not improve the quality of other indebtedness.

General Obligation Bonds

General obligation bonds are long-term state and local debt on which the issuing unit pledges as security its full faith and credit. In addition, the issuing unit must have the power to levy taxes at any level necessary in order to meet debt service payments. There are, however, practical limits beyond which taxes cannot be collected successfully. The basic security of this type of bond is necessarily based upon the economic resources of the taxpayers in the issuing unit.

The main controversy in this description is just how broad the issuing unit's taxing power should be before long-term debts are classified as general obligations. In this study general obligations are bonds for the service of which the issuing state or local unit has pledged its entire tax revenues. The issuing unit must either be able to levy property taxes for bond service payments at an unlimited level or have the power to levy property taxes (even if only at a limited level) and at least one other type of tax for bond service payments at an unlimited level.

Described in this manner, the general obligation category includes several forms of state and local debt which are sometimes classified separately. These include: (1) state and local debt for which the issuing unit can levy only a limited level of property taxes but can levy one or more other types of taxes at an unlimited level; (2) unlimited special assessment bonds, i.e., state and local bonds for which there is no limit on the rate or amount of property tax that can be levied on benefiting property for the payment of the bonds; and (3) hybrid types of state and local bonds payable primarily from pledged revenues or receipts from limited revenues or from limited or special taxes, but for which the issuing unit pledges its full faith, credit and taxing power if these limited sources fall short.

The measurement of the quality of general obligation bonds as a separate category of state and local debt is difficult because the needed information is not available at the present time. It is clearly improper to compare the service charges on general obligations alone with the cash resources to meet debt service charges developed in Chapter 5 or with state and local general revenues. This incomparability is because large portions of state and local revenues are restricted in their use to the servicing of limited liability obligations or guaranteed debt or are earmarked to be used for specific purposes only. A sizable portion of state and local cash and near-cash balances are also restricted in use by the same methods. The measures most helpful in assessing the quality of general obligations separately are unrestricted general revenues and unrestricted cash flows and balances which can be used to service such obligations. The unused state and local taxing capacity and the willingness of the federal government to assist financially distressed state and local units would

TABLE 17

Cash Coverage of the Debt Service Charges on Revenue Bonds in 1963, 1965 and 1967

Cash Flow Coverage of Debt Service Charges	All Revenue Bonds Studied			Toll Road Revenue Bonds			Total Excl. Toll Issues		
	Number	Per Cent	Cum. %[a]	Number	Per Cent	Cum. %[a]	Number	Per Cent	Cum. %[a]
1963									
.00- .74	23	1.7	1.7	15	15.0	15.0	8	.6	.6
.75- .99	54	4.0	5.7	13	13.0	28.0	41	3.3	3.9
1.00-1.24	175	12.9	18.6	23	23.0	51.0	152	12.1	16.0
1.25-1.49	225	16.6	35.2	14	14.0	65.0	211	16.8	32.8
1.50-1.74	238	17.5	52.7	9	9.0	74.0	229	18.3	51.1
1.75-1.99	162	12.0	64.7	6	6.0	80.0	156	12.4	63.5
2.00-2.49	198	14.6	79.3	3	3.0	83.0	195	15.5	79.0
2.50-2.99	117	8.6	87.9	5	5.0	88.0	112	8.9	87.9
3.00-3.99	71	5.2	93.1	6	6.0	94.0	65	5.2	93.1
4.00-4.99	45	3.4	96.5	3	3.0	97.0	42	3.4	96.5
5.00 & above	47	3.5	100.0	3	3.0	100.0	44	3.5	100.0
1963 totals	1,355	100.0		100	100.0		1,255	100.0	
1965									
.00- .74	15	.7	.9	10	11.2	11.2	5	.3	.3
.75- .99	39	2.3	3.2	7	7.9	19.1	32	2.0	2.3
1.00-1.24	235	13.7	16.9	17	19.1	38.2	218	13.4	15.7
1.25-1.49	405	23.5	40.4	10	11.2	49.4	395	24.2	39.9
1.50-1.74	283	16.4	56.8	13	14.6	64.0	270	16.5	56.4
1.75-1.99	211	12.3	69.1	11	12.4	76.4	200	12.3	68.7
2.00-2.49	229	13.3	82.4	8	9.0	85.4	221	13.5	82.2
2.50-2.99	102	5.9	88.3	3	3.4	88.8	99	6.1	88.3
3.00-3.99	110	6.3	94.6	6	6.7	95.5	104	6.4	94.7
4.00-4.99	31	1.8	96.4	1	1.1	96.6	30	1.8	96.5
5.00 & above	61	3.6	100.0	3	3.4	100.0	58	3.5	100.0
1965 totals	1,721	100.0		89	100.0		1,632	100.0	

(continued)

TABLE 17 concluded

Cash Flow Coverage of Debt Service Charges	All Revenue Bonds Studied			Toll Road Revenue Bonds			Total Excl. Toll Issues		
	Number	Per Cent	Cum. %[a]	Number	Per Cent	Cum. %[a]	Number	Per Cent	Cum. %[a]
1967									
.00-.74	12	.6	.6	10	12.3	12.3	2	.1	.1
.75-.99	35	1.8	2.4	10	12.3	24.7	25	1.4	1.5
1.00-1.24	318	16.6	19.0	9	11.1	35.8	309	16.8	18.3
1.25-1.49	435	22.7	41.6	16	19.8	55.6	419	22.8	41.1
1.50-1.74	344	17.9	59.5	8	9.9	65.4	336	18.3	59.3
1.75-1.99	215	11.2	70.7	6	7.4	72.8	209	11.4	70.7
2.00-2.49	260	13.5	84.3	12	14.8	87.6	248	13.5	84.2
2.50-2.99	100	5.2	89.5	2	2.4	90.1	98	5.3	89.5
3.00-3.99	99	5.2	94.7	5	6.2	96.2	94	5.1	94.6
4.00-4.99	38	2.0	96.7	2	2.4	98.7	36	2.0	96.6
5.00 & above	63	3.3	100.0	1	1.2	100.0	62	3.4	100.0
1967 totals	1,919	100.0		81	100.0		1,838	100.0	

Source: Municipal Bond Selector by Standard and Poor's Corporation, February 27, 1964, February 28, 1966, and February 28, 1968.

[a]Indicates cumulative percentage at or below highest cash coverage in row.

also be very useful information. Unfortunately the above types of information are not available at the present time. In the author's opinion, therefore, the best method currently available to assess the quality of general obligations is to compare over-all state and local debt service charges with over-all cash resources available to meet these debt service charges as was done in Chapter 5.

Summary

The characteristics for the categories of state and local debt classified by type of governmental unit showed that incorporated municipalities and special districts had much higher debt burdens than other types of units. Instruments and borrower characteristics for units in statewide geographic regions demonstrated that some areas had much heavier debt burdens; however, the states with heavier burdens were spread throughout the United States and changed over time. The impact of changes in quality among these categories on the over-all quality of state and local debt does not seem very large.

Classification by type of resources used to pay debt service charges proved to be the most fruitful classification in analyzing the over-all quality of state and local debt. Federally guaranteed debt has remained a constant proportion of all state and local debt over the postwar period; however, so have liquid assets and other measures of the ability to repay such debt. There is, therefore, no evidence in these two categories of any significant changes in quality over the postwar period. By far the most rapid relative and absolute increase in state and local debt was in the limited liability obligation category. The cash flow coverage of the debt service charges on such indebtedness has improved moderately in the last decade; however, the increased absolute and relative amounts of limited liability obligations outstanding may weaken the over-all quality of state and local debt. The security behind most limited liability obligations is weaker than full faith and credit debt. The postwar payment record is poorer for limited liability obligations than for general obligations. Furthermore, since all revenues from the pledged source are usually restricted to one specific project or purpose, the residual unrestricted revenues probably cover general obligation debt service charges to a smaller extent than before the rapid postwar growth in limited liability obligations.

7

EVALUATIONS BY RATING AGENCIES

Ratings are assigned to many state and local bond issues by the major rating services. These ratings are determined by experienced bond analysts and are based on their assessment both of instrument and borrower characteristics and of changes in the external environment in which the issue will exist. When the ratings assigned to state and local issues are aggregated, the movements in the aggregate distributions should provide the rating agencies' evaluation of prospective quality.

In this chapter, the meaning and application of the rating classifications used are reviewed. Some of the characteristics that the rating agencies use and the historical record of ratings are briefly examined. Then, percentage distributions of the number and dollar amount of state and local debt outstanding and issued annually in each rating category are analyzed.

The Meaning and Use of Agency Ratings

Three companies — Moody's Investors Service, Inc., Standard and Poor's Corporation, and Dun and Bradstreet, Inc. — have rated state and local issues in recent years. All three agencies emphasize the fact that they grade individual issues of state and local units in terms of credit risk and do not consider the investment merits of the issue in rating decisions. Dun and Bradstreet has generally confined its analysis to a limited number of large issues, while Moody's Investors Service, Inc., and Standard and Poor's Corporation classify a much broader category of securities. Table 18 shows that Moody's has rated approximately two-thirds of the dollar amount of state and local debt outstanding in the postwar period. Moody's or Standard and Poor's have rated slightly over three-fourths of the dollar amount of newly issued state and local debt. Table 18 also shows that a substantially higher proportion of

TABLE 18

Proportionate Dollar Amounts of Long-Term State and Local Debt
Outstanding and Newly Issued Which Are Rated

Year of Manual	Percentage of Long-Term Debt Rated	Percentage of General Obligations Rated	Percentage of Limited Liability Obligations Rated	Rated Limited Liability Obligations As Per Cent of All Rated Debt
Long-Term State and Local Debt Outstanding^a				
1943^b	77.0	85.4	25.6	4.7
1949	73.7	73.7	73.5	10.6
1952	70.2	73.7	52.4	12.3
1954	73.2	81.2	48.4	16.0
1956	67.3	77.6	43.8	20.0
1958	65.7	83.0	33.6	18.0
1960	64.3	74.2	46.5	25.9
1966	67.5	82.3	45.4	27.0
Long-Term Newly Issued State and Local Debt^c				
1957-58	76.3	83.5	55.9	19.0
1959	78.2	86.7	61.0	25.6
1960	72.4	84.0	45.8	19.2
1961	77.7	91.7	46.8	18.7
1962	78.9	89.5	55.3	21.8
1963	76.0	84.2	63.5	33.4
1964	78.5	90.8	55.4	25.4
1965	79.3	90.8	55.9	23.2
1966	75.4	89.1	51.9	25.3
1967	80.0	93.2	56.3	25.1
1968	84.1	92.2	71.9	34.2
1957-68^d	78.6	88.9	57.9	25.2

Sources: Data from Moody's Investors Service, Inc. and the Investment Bankers Association.

^{a}Dollar value rated by Moody's Investors Service.

^{b}Issues of $200,000 or over; for all other years for issues of $600,000 or over.

^{c}Dollar value rated by Moody's Investors Service, by Standard and Poor's Corporation or by both.

^{d}The figures in these rows are totals or percentages of totals for the period listed.

general obligations are rated as compared to limited liability obligations.[1]

In this study the rating classification of Moody's Investors Service are used because Moody's began publishing ratings for a sizeable proportion of the bonds outstanding as early as 1919 and because the Investment Bankers Association uses the Moody's rating for its rating information on new state and local issues.[2] Moody's describes its rating symbols in the following manner (descriptions condensed):

Aaa—bonds with the smallest degree of investment risk, interest payments are protected by a large or by an exceptionally stable margin and principal is secure; changes in various protective elements are most unlikely to impair the fundamentally strong position of such issues.

Aa—high quality of all standards but rated lower than best bonds because of lower margins of protection, greater amplitude of fluctuations of protective elements or some other elements which make the long-term risk appear somewhat larger than on the best bonds.

A—higher medium grade obligations with adequate factors given security to principal and interest but with elements present which suggest a susceptibility to impairment sometime in the future.

Baa—lower medium grade bonds which are neither highly protected nor poorly secured; interest payments and principal appear adequate for the present but certain protective elements may be lacking or may be characteristically unreliable over any great length of time.

Ba—bonds whose future cannot be considered as well assured; usually the protection of interest and principal may be very moderate and thereby not well safeguarded during both good and bad times over the future.

B—bonds where the assurance of interest and principal payments or of maintenance of other terms of the contract over any long period of time may be small.

[1]Figures are not available for the proportionate dollar amount of state and local debt outstanding that is rated by Standard and Poor's. Since the total number of state and local issues outstanding is not available, the proportionate number of rated issues cannot be computed. Unpublished figures furnished by the Investment Bankers Association indicate that slightly less than 50 per cent of the total number of long-term state and local issues from 1957 through 1968 were rated by Moody's or Standard and Poor's. Representatives of Moody's and Standard and Poor's gave three reasons for not rating state and local issues: (1) issues of units where debt outstanding is less than a specified amount ($600,000 for Moody's) or was sold privately; (2) issues that are not rated as a matter of policy, e.g., real estate bonds; and (3) issues where data essential for sound rating judgment is missing.

[2]Dun and Bradstreet rates a substantially smaller number of issues and Standard and Poor's did not begin rating state and local debt until the early 1950's. While the opinions of these rating services differ on specific issues, the over-all rating distributions are quite similar (see George H. Hempel, "The Postwar Quality of Municipal Bonds," p. 200).

Caa—bonds of poor standing which are in default or contain present elements of danger with respect to principal or interest.

Ca—bonds which are speculative in a high degree; such issues are in default or have other marked shortcomings.

C—lowest rated class of bonds; have extremely poor prospects of ever attaining any real investment standing.[3]

The percentage distributions in this section include distribution for both the dollar value and the number of rated long-term state and local debts outstanding at a point in time and the same figures for rated long-term debt issued during a particular time period. The distinction between and the comparability of these two types of rating distributions should be understood before one analyzes the rating agency's assessment of instrument and borrower characteristics and of changes in the external environment.

Typically, there is only one rating for all long-term general obligations of a particular state or local governmental unit and for all long-term issues of a specific revenue project. Some governmental units or revenue projects have more than one rating because special security is pledged for some of the bonds. New issues of a previously rated unit or revenue project are usually assigned the same rating as the outstanding debt unless there are material changes in the credit situation. Therefore, new issues of a previously rated unit or revenue project usually increase the dollar value outstanding in a rating category but usually do not affect the number of state and local issues in a rating category. The serial retirement of most long-term state and local debt is also reflected by a decline in the dollar value of long-term debt outstanding but not in the number of issues outstanding. Finally, changes in the rating of state and local bonds after they are issued are reflected in both the number and dollar value of long-term state and local debt outstanding in a specific rating classification. The distributions based on the number and dollar value of rated debt outstanding should provide an accurate profile of the rating agency's evaluation of the quality of all rated long-term state and local debt at that time.

Rating distributions based on long-term debt issued during a particular time period reflect both the number and dollar value of each new issue that is rated. Some governmental units may have several new issues with the same rating in a single time period. Each of these issues is reflected in the rating distributions by dollar value and number issued. The ratings reflected in these distributions are those assigned at the time of issue and neither retirements nor rating changes affect these distributions. The rating distributions based on the number and dollar value of rated debt issued should give an indication of

[3]Moody's Investors Service, Inc., *Moody's Municipal and Government Manual*, New York, 1969, p. vi.

movements in the rating agency's evaluation of the quality of rated long-term state and local debt.

Because of the differences discussed in the preceding paragraphs, the rating distributions of long-term state and local debt outstanding should not be compared directly with the rating distributions of long-term and local debt issued. This seems particularly true for rating distributions based on the number of state and local bonds outstanding and on the number of newly issued bonds, since the two types of distributions are based on noncomparable data. Limited comparisons seem permissible when dollar value outstanding and the dollar value issued are based upon reasonably comparable data. Possible rating changes after the bonds are issued and possible maturity differences within rating categories limit the significance of a comparison between the rating distributions based on the dollar value outstanding and those based on the dollar value issued.

Another possible limit to comparability of rating distributions based on the two methods used here is the advent of bonds with Public Housing Authority contracts in 1951. These Public Housing Authority bonds are all rated Aaa. Thus, if they are included in the rating distributions, they tend to improve average bond quality. Since these bonds are guaranteed by the federal government, many bond analysts feel they should be treated as federal rather than state and local debt. The rating distributions of outstanding long-term state and local debt studied here do not include Public Housing Authority bonds because the raw data available for the purpose of analysis exclude these bonds. In contrast, the raw data on rated long-term state and local debt issued include Public Housing Authority bonds. In this study the rating distributions for rated long-term debt issued are presented both including and excluding Public Housing Authority bonds.

Characteristics Considered by Rating Agencies

Before analyzing the percentage distributions of rated long-term state and local debt, one should be aware of the processes followed and characteristics considered in assigning a rating to an issue and of the past payment performance of rated issues.

The processes used by the two agencies rating a high proportion of state and local bonds, Moody's Investors Service and Standard and Poor's Corporation, generally consist of two steps.[4] First, all of the pertinent characteristics about the issuing unit or the project being financed is gathered and investigat-

---

[4]The rating process used by Dun and Bradstreet involves a smaller number of analysts and is more formalized. The characteristics considered by Dun and Bradstreet also seem to be similar to those formulated in the conceptual model in Chapter 2.

ed by an experienced bond analyst. Most of these analysts specialize in geographic areas or particular types of revenue-producing projects. Second, a rating committee considers all of the data collected by the analyst until the committee members reach substantial agreement on the appropriate rating category. The rating committee typically consists of the analyst who prepares the data, several senior analysts, an investment counselor and any other member of the rating agency who has intimate knowledge about the area or project being evaluated. Most new issues that meet the agency's minimum prerequisites for being rated are assigned to a rating category. If the governmental unit has similar issues which have already been rated, the examination of the new issue is usually perfunctory and the same rating is assigned to it unless there is evidence of any fundamental change in the situation.

When interviewed, representatives of Moody's and Standard and Poor's state that their respective agencies used instrument and borrower characteristics similar to those discussed in the conceptual model in Chapter 2 and used in this study. These representatives were then asked about the standards (or desired levels) for instrument and borrower characteristics in a rating category and about the weights applied to these characteristics or groups of characteristics. The answer in both cases was that neither the specific analyst nor the rating committees have formal standards or weights for instrument or borrower charactistics or groups of such characteristics. The effect of the future external environment was also considered in an informal manner. The representatives of both rating agencies seemed to feel that purely objective measurements were not appropriate for selecting the rating category of a state and local issue. Instead, they emphasized the importance of careful study and decisions made by experienced bond analysts and committees.[5]

Results from two past analyses of the instrument and borrower characteristics affecting the ratings assigned to state and local issues supported the agency's statements that they used characteristics similar to those in the

---

[5]In the author's opinion there are several factors which support such a nonmechanistic evaluation of instrument and borrower characteristics and the future external environment to determine the ratings assigned to state and local issues. First, the instrument and borrower characteristics should be analyzed in conjunction with each other rather than separate measures. Second, many measures affecting the quality of an issue, e.g., the future economic environment, cannot be accurately expressed in quantitative terms. Third, various rating analysts may give different weights to characteristics and to interrelationships among characteristics, and these weights may change as conditions change.

On the other hand, the agencies' present nonmechanistic evaluation of instrument and borrower characteristics and the future external environment has several disadvantages. First, the characteristics that decide the ratings of state and local issues are largely uncontrollable. Second, the weights given to characteristics might be shifted unconsciously among different rating situations. Third, there is no assurance that final rating decisions are consistent over longer periods of time. Finally, it is more difficult for interested persons (like the author) to use and assess agency ratings.

conceptual model formulated and used in this study.

Carleton and Lerner used multiple discriminant analysis[6] to test the effect of six simple characteristics (debt to assessed values, debt to population, log population, log debt, average collection rate and school district or not) on the ratings of general obligations. Their analysis showed: (1) the means of the characteristics they studied were ordered among bond ratings in the fashion predicted by the conceptual model; (2) the signs of the weights that most effectively discriminated between the various ratings were consistent with the conceptual model; and (3) using discriminate function weights and knowledge of the rating distribution for the sample, Carleton and Lerner were able to predict the actual ratings in 53 per cent of the cases and within one rating category in an additional 40 per cent of the cases.[7]

In the second test, the author used multiple correlation analysis[8] to test the linear relationships between twenty-three instrument and borrower characteristics (all of the quantitative characteristics available at the time of the study) and a selected sample of general obligations. The sample was selected by randomly choosing twenty general obligations in each of the top four rating categories from all the larger issues in that category that had maintained the same rating from 1949 through 1963. The results of this analysis demonstrated that the means of nearly all of the characteristics studied were ordered among bond ratings in the manner predicted by the conceptual model in both 1949 and 1963.[9]

Linear regression equations based on five characteristics, selected by factor analysis to limit multicollinearity (estimated true property value to over-all tax supported debt, percentage of property taxes uncollected, deviation from average population change in the preceding seven years, over-all tax supported debt as a per cent of disposable personal income and the nonwhite proportion of the population) explained approximately 55 per cent of the rating differences in 1949 and approximately 39 per cent in 1963. The signs of the coefficients of the five characteristics were consistent with the conceptual model. The regression equations were good rating predictors for other samples in the same year. The coefficients of the five characteristics did change

[6]A multivariate statistical technique designed to assign weights to several characteristics in a manner so that the characteristics studied have the maximum ability to predict into which of several different credit classifications a bond issue will fall.

[7]Willard T. Carleton and Eugene M. Lerner, "Statistical Credit Scoring of Municipal Bonds," an unpublished research report financed by the Federal Deposit Insurance Corporation, Washington, D.C.

[8]A multivariate statistical test used to measure the extent and nature of the linear relationship between a dependent variable and two or more relatively independent variables.

[9]George H. Hempel, "Postwar Quality of Municipal Bonds," pp. 226-235.

between 1949 and 1963, however, and the 1949 equation was a relatively poor predictor for 1963 ratings.[10]

Past Payment Performance of Rated State and Local Issues

One method which is useful in assessing how well ratings measure prospective quality is an analysis of the past payment performance of rated state and local issues. The ratings of 264 state and local units which defaulted during the 1929 depression period and of the 6 postwar default situations that had rated issues are examined in the following paragraphs.

Table 19 summarizes the 1929 rating distributions for 264 state and local units which defaulted during the 1929 depression period. The 264 units include the general obligations of all defaulting states, all defaulting incorporated municipalities and school districts with a 1930 population of over 10,000, all counties with a 1930 population of over 50,000, and all other districts with a 1930 population of over 25,000. The Seattle Street Railway issue was the only defaulting revenue bond rated in 1929. It was rated Baa, but is not included in Table 19. While the 264 defaulted issues in Table 19 seem relatively small when compared to the total number of defaults, the dollar value of these issues is over three-fourths of the total amount of defaulted state and local debt in that period.

The proportionate totals in Table 19 show that 78 per cent of the defaulting issues were rated Aa or better in 1929. The defaulting issues rated Aa or better in 1929 constituted 94.4 per cent of the total dollar value of the 264 issues. Many of the bonds rated A or below were the debts of Florida municipal units which had experienced financial difficulties before 1929. The large proportion of defaulting state and local issues in the top rating categories appears to be partly explained by the large percentage of issues in the top rating categories in 1929 — 53 per cent of all rated issues were rated Aaa, 24 per cent were rated Aa, 18 per cent were rated A, and 5 per cent were rated Baa or lower. Furthermore, the ratings at that time appear biased in favor of large governmental units. Nearly 98 per cent of the 310 cities with populations of over 30,000 were rated Aa or better. Nevertheless, it is disturbing that such a high proportion of the 264 defaulting issues were rated Aa or better in 1929.

Chart 20 was formulated to demonstrate what happened to the ratings of the 264 defaulting units from 1926-37. Unfortunately, the only year in this period for which there is an over-all rating count is 1929. Chart 20 reveals that the quality of this group of issues as assessed by the rating agency began

___

[10]*Ibid.* When asked about the changes in the coefficients of the characteristics, representatives of the two major rating agencies stated that some nonmeasurable factors had changed appreciably between the two periods. The two factors specifically cited were: the improvements in the quality of state and local financial administration and the much greater predicted stability for economic activity.

TABLE 19

1929 Ratings for Bonds Which Defaulted During the 1929 Depression Period

1929 Moody's Rating	States	Cities and Towns[a]	School Districts[a]	Counties[b]	Other Districts[c]	Total	Percentage of Total
Based on Number of Issues							
Aaa	1	67	31	25	3	127	48.1
Aa	—	46	18	15	—	79	29.9
A	—	16	3	5	—	24	9.1
Baa	—	5	1	2	—	8	3.0
Nonrated	—	9	12	2	3	26	9.9
Total	1	143	65	49	6	264	100.0
Based on Par Value of Issues (in millions of dollars)							
Aaa	160.3	1,021.9	130.6	229.6	247.0	1,789.4	78.8
Aa	—	258.0	26.0	69.0	—	353.0	15.6
A	—	47.3	3.4	16.6	—	67.3	3.0
Baa	—	25.8	1.3	9.7	—	36.8	1.6
Nonrated	—	2.3	5.7	.3	13.9	22.2	1.0
Total	160.3	1,355.3	167.0	325.2	260.9	2,268.7	100.0

Source: Unpublished list of names and par values by *The Daily Bond Buyer.*

[a]With populations over 10,000 in 1930 census.

[b]With populations over 50,000 in 1930 census.

[c]With populations over 25,000 in 1930 census.

CHART 20
Percentage Rating Distributions of 264 Defaulting Bonds, 1926-37

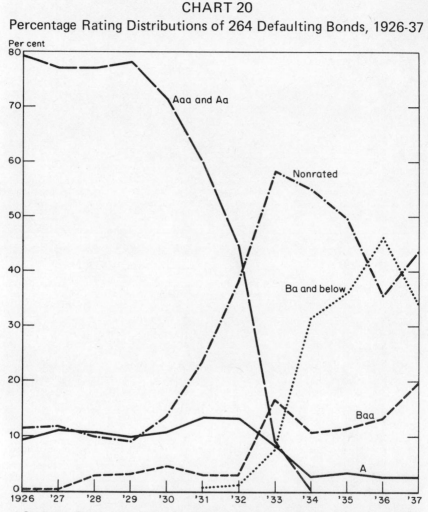

Per cent

Aaa and Aa

Nonrated

Ba and below

Baa

A

1926 '27 '28 '29 '30 '31 '32 '33 '34 '35 '36 '37

Sources: Rating information from Moody's Investors Service *Manuals,* 1925-38. Default data from NBER files based on data from *The Bond Buyer,* Investment Bankers Association, Dun & Bradstreet, Moody's Investors Service, etc.

declining appreciably in 1931, the first year state and local default situtations became widespread. By 1934, when nearly all of the defaults had occurred, the rating distribution reflected the very weak quality of these 264 state and local units. This reflection would not have been of much benefit to the investor who bought one of the "high quality" Aaa or Aa rated issues in 1931.

Another type of analysis was applied to the same group of defaulting units. The rating of these units in each year from five years before the year of

TABLE 20

Rating Distributions of State and Local Debt Issues Which Defaulted in the 1929-37 Period

Rating	5 Yrs. Before Yr. of Default	4 Yrs. Before Yr. of Default	3 Yrs. Before Yr. of Default	2 Yrs. Before Yr. of Default	1 Yr. Before Yr. of Default	Year of Default	Year After Default
Aaa	95	92	83	68	33	8	
Aa	50	52	52	47	46	16	2
A	16	15	17	29	26	16	4
Baa	3	3	6	6	20	41	27
Ba		1	3	5	8	12	35
B						5	23
Caa & below							1
Nonrated	13	14	16	22	44	79	85
Total	177	177	177	177	177	177	177

Note: The 264 largest default situations were studied; however, accurate date of default information was not available on 87 of these situations.

Source: Rating information from Moody's Investors Service *Manuals*, 1925-38. Default data from NBER files which are based on data from *The Bond Buyer*, Investment Bankers Association, Dun and Bradstreet, Moody's Investors Service, etc.

default to the year following default are summarized in Table 20. The data in Table 20 show that the rating agencies begin to recognize the probability of default for significant numbers of the units beginning approximately one year before the unit defaulted. The number of Aaa or Aa rated issues was still 44.1 per cent of all the defaulting issues in the year prior to default. Unfortunately, we do not have sufficient data at this time to analyze how much of a downward rating shift occurred in nondefaulting units during similar time periods.

Two qualifications should be made to any conclusion arising from the analysis of the rating distributions of the 264 defaulting units. First, most of the issues studied did not have any final loss of interest or principal. If the investors were able to wait out the depression period, they usually suffered no final loss. Second, as a result of the depression and default experience in this period, substantial adjustments have been made in the way state and local issues are rated. For example, large size is no longer considered synonymous with high quality. It is also no longer assumed that all taxes levied will be collected. Because of these and similar adjustments, many analysts believe that ratings assigned to state and local issues before the mid-1930's are not comparable with those assigned after that time.

Only six rated state and local issues have defaulted since the 1929 major default period. All six were limited liability obligations and five of the six issues were rated for the first time by Moody's Investors Service in January 1958. At that time the revenue bonds of the West Virginia Turnpike Commission, the revenue bonds of the Burt County Bridge Commission and the Parkersburg Bridge Revenue Bonds were rated Caa. At approximately the same time, the Dunbar Bridge Revenue Bonds and the revenue bonds of the Bellevue Bridge Commission were rated Ca. The Calumet Skyway Toll Bridge Revenue Bonds were rated Caa by Moody's Investors Service in August 1963. The ratings of these six defaulting issues have not been changed since they were first rated by Moody's.

Three of these six limited liability obligations were rated by Moody's after they had defaulted. The revenue bonds of the Bellevue Bridge Commission and the Burt County Bridge Commission had been in default for several years before they were rated. The Calumet Skyway Revenue Bonds were rated for the first time approximately a month after their default. It was impossible for agency ratings to be indicative of these three default situations. It might even be argued that these cases illustrate that unrated state and local issues are more likely to default than rated issues. However, the revenue bonds of the West Virginia Turnpike Commission and of the Dunbar and Parkersburg bridges defaulted from several months to two years after Moody's rated them. One of the primary reasons for the differences in the timing of ratings is that the earnings records were available for the West Virginia Turnpike, Dunbar Bridge and Parkersburg Bridge revenue bond situations for several years before they defaulted. Thus, financial records as well as agency ratings had forecasted low quality before the defaults occurred.

The most favorable conclusion one can derive from the past payment performance of rated state and local issues is that the new and more sophisticated rating processes started in the mid-1930's (after the weak performance before the mid-1930's) are largely untested as an indicator of prospective quality. In spite of the lack of historical proof, the consensus opinions of groups of sophisticated bond analysts (i.e., agency ratings) are analyzed as meaningful indicators of prospective quality.

Aggregated Rating Distributions

The percentage distributions by rating categories based on the number of outstanding long-term state and local bonds rated by Moody's Investors Service for most years from 1938 through 1969 are presented in Table 21. These rating distributions indicate that the quality of rated state and local bonds improved considerably during World War II and the years immediately thereafter. For instance, the proportionate number of outstanding rated state and local bonds classified as Aaa or Aa rose from 10.5 per cent in 1938 to 29.4 per cent in 1950. Over the same period, the proportion of rated state and local bonds classified as Ba or below fell from 19.2 per cent to 8.8 per cent.

Throughout the 1950's the quality of rated long-term state and local debt as indicated by the distributions of the number of rated bonds outstanding appears to have remained relatively stable. Since the late 1950's, however, the rating distributions in Table 21 suggest that the quality of rated long-term state and local debt may have deteriorated slightly. The proportion of state and local bonds rated A or Baa increased throughout the 1950-69 period. The proportion of bonds rated Ba or below declined in the 1950's; however, this decline was approximately offset by the similar decrease in the proportion of bonds rated Aaa or Aa in that decade. Since the late 1950's, the decline in the proportion of bonds rated Aaa or Aa has continued, but there was little change in the number of bonds rated Ba or lower. The rating distributions in Table 21, therefore, appear to indicate that the over-all quality of rated long-term state and local debt had deteriorated moderately in the 1960's. This slight deterioration was caused by a movement from the high rating categories (Aaa and Aa) into the medium rating categories (A or Baa) rather than to an increase in the relative number of issues rated Ba or below.

The rating distributions of the number of rated state and local bonds issued from 1957 through 1968 are presented in Table 22. The proportionate number of newly issued bonds that were classified as A remained fairly constant throughout the 1957-68 period. The proportion of newly issued bonds that were classified as Aaa or Aa fell slowly from 1957 through 1965, while those classified as Baa and Ba or below increased in this same period. The decreasing proportion in the higher rating categories and the increasing proportion in the lower rating categories indicate that the quality of newly issued

TABLE 21

Percentage Distribution of Rated State and Local Debt
Outstanding, by Number of Issuers
(per cent in rating category)

Year of Manual	Aaa	Aa	A	Baa	Ba	B	Below B
1938[a]	1.5	9.0	40.4	29.8	13.5	3.7	2.0
1939[a]	1.2	14.3	39.2	29.0	11.5	3.3	1.4
1943[a]	1.6	16.0	38.4	28.9	10.0	3.9	1.3
1947[a]	5.7	23.8	38.5	20.4	6.9	3.5	1.2
1948[a]	4.8	23.2	38.7	24.3	5.4	2.5	1.0
1949	5.6	23.1	37.2	23.7	6.5	2.9	1.0
1950	5.6	23.8	38.2	23.7	5.7	2.2	.9
1951	4.6	24.7	39.4	23.3	5.2	2.2	.7
1952	4.3	22.7	39.6	24.9	5.5	2.3	.7
1953	3.8	24.2	40.3	23.9	6.3	1.3	.1
1954	3.9	23.3	40.7	26.5	4.5	1.1	.1
1955	3.3	21.6	44.7	25.4	4.1	.8	.1
1956	3.1	20.9	46.6	25.5	3.3	.6	.1
1957	2.8	19.6	47.5	26.7	2.8	.5	.0[b]
1958	2.8	20.1	47.4	26.7	2.4	.4	.1
1959	2.6	18.6	47.3	28.4	2.7	.3	.1
1960	2.4	16.7	46.0	31.5	3.0	.3	.1
1961	2.3	17.0	47.6	29.6	3.1	.2	.1
1962	2.3	16.2	47.9	30.4	2.9	.2	.1
1963	2.3	15.7	47.2	31.6	2.8	.3	.1
1964	2.9	13.9	49.0	31.4	2.5	.3	.1
1965	3.0	13.9	48.3	31.9	2.5	.4	.1
1966	3.0	14.1	47.4	32.5	2.6	.4	.1
1967	3.5	13.1	47.1	33.5	2.4	.3	.1
1968	3.4	12.4	48.3	33.3	2.2	.3	.1
1969	3.1	14.1	46.9	33.4	2.1	.3	.1

Note: Public Housing Authority bonds are not included. Rows may not add up to 100.0 per cent because of rounding.

Source: Unpublished information from Moody's Investors Service, Inc. Rating count for 1962, 1964, 1965, 1966, 1967, 1968 and 1969 were made by the National Bureau of Economic Research staff.

[a]Issues of $200,000 or over; for all other years of issues of $600,000 or over.

[b]Amount less than .05 per cent.

TABLE 22

Percentage Distributions of Rated Long-Term State and Local
Bonds Issued, by Number of Issues in Year of Issue
(per cent in rating category)

Year	Aaa	Aa	A	Baa	Ba & Below
Including Public Housing Bonds					
1957	8.2	27.4	43.1	19.4	1.9
1958	7.9	25.7	42.6	21.7	2.1
1959	8.4	24.1	41.3	23.9	2.2
1960	9.0	22.6	41.7	24.2	2.5
1961	7.7	22.1	43.1	24.5	2.6
1962	8.6	21.0	43.5	24.3	2.6
1963	6.2	20.3	42.4	27.9	3.2
1964	8.5	19.9	41.8	27.0	2.8
1965	7.6	18.8	42.3	28.0	3.2
1966	9.2	21.3	40.1	26.7	2.7
1967	8.1	20.2	41.1	28.5	2.3
1968	7.4	18.2	44.0	28.1	2.3
Excluding Public Housing Bonds					
1957	6.6	27.8	43.9	19.8	1.9
1958	4.1	26.7	44.4	22.6	2.2
1959	5.6	24.8	42.6	24.7	2.2
1960	5.9	23.4	43.1	25.0	2.6
1961	3.8	23.0	44.9	25.6	2.7
1962	5.0	21.8	45.2	25.3	2.7
1963	4.2	20.7	43.4	28.4	3.3
1964	3.7	20.9	44.0	28.4	3.0
1965	3.8	19.4	44.2	29.2	3.3
1966	4.0	22.5	42.3	28.2	2.8
1967	3.8	21.1	42.9	29.8	2.4
1968	3.2	19.1	46.0	29.4	2.4

Note: Rows may not add up to 100.0 per cent because of rounding.

Source: Data from the Investment Bankers Association.

rated long-term state and local debt deteriorated slightly in the period from 1957 through 1965. The distributions in Table 22 also indicate that the quality of newly issued rated long-term bonds remained relatively stable in 1966 and 1967, then appeared to deteriorate slightly again in 1968.

When aggregate quality is emphasized, the percentage rating distributions based on the dollar value of outstanding and newly issued rated long-term state and local debt are probably more significant than similar distributions based on the number of rated issuers or issues. The distributions based on number are primarily useful as an indication of the quality of smaller rated issuers or issues. The rating distributions of the dollar value of rated long-term debt outstanding at several intervals from 1938 through 1966 appear in Table 23. These rating distributions indicate that the quality of rated state and local bonds outstanding improved during the postwar period until the mid-1950's, remained relatively stable in the mid- and late-1950's, then deteriorated moderately in the 1960-66 period. The proportion of rated state and local bonds

TABLE 23

Percentage Distributions of Rated State and Local Debt Outstanding,
by Dollar Value of Debt Outstanding
(per cent in rating category)

Year of Manual	Value of Rated Bonds ($ millions)	Aaa	Aa	A	Baa	Ba	B & Below
1938	14,507[a]	6.9	17.4	47.9	19.9	5.5	2.5
1939	15,914[a]	7.5	17.4	48.1	20.7	4.3	2.1
1943	14,179[a]	8.1	17.0	48.4	21.2	3.7	1.5
1947	15,067[a]	10.8	18.2	52.9	13.1	3.0	2.1
1949	13,312	8.1	25.7	52.1	11.1	2.5	.5
1952	17,939	10.2	26.0	49.5	11.8	1.9	.6
1954	23,441	11.7	30.5	45.1	10.6	1.7	.4
1956	28,428	11.7	28.8	47.1	10.6	1.6	.3
1958	33,402	9.9	28.4	48.7	11.5	1.3	.2
1960	39,303	11.8	33.3	36.5	16.5	1.5	.5
1966	63,599	8.5	27.8	41.2	19.4	2.3	.8

Note: Public Housing Authority bonds, which are rated, are not included. Rows may not add up to 100.0 per cent because of rounding.

Source: Unpublished information from Moody's Investors Service, Inc. Rating count for 1966 by NBER staff.

[a]Issues of $200,000 or over; for all other years for issues of $600,000 or over.

outstanding that were rated Aaa or Aa is higher and the proportion rated Baa or below is lower for the later years covered in Table 23. The primary deviation from this pattern was the 1960-66 period when the proportion rated Aaa or Aa declined and the proportion rated Baa or below increased.

The rating distributions for the dollar value of long-term state and local debt issued annually from 1945 through 1968 are presented in Table 24. When Public Housing Authority bonds are included, the rating distributions indicate that the quality of newly issued bonds improved moderately from the mid-1940's through the mid-1950's. The data in Table 24 indicate that when Public Housing bonds are included, the quality of rated bonds issued in the mid- and late-1940's seems roughly the same as the quality of the same bonds issued in the mid-1960's.

When Public Housing Authority bonds are not included, the rating distributions in Table 24 indicate that the quality of newly issued rated bonds remained constant from the mid-1940's through the mid-1950's, then deteriorated in the late 1950's and the 1960's. The most noticeable change in the late 1950's and early 1960's was the shift from the Aaa and Aa rating categories into the A and Baa rating categories. In the mid-1960's the shift was from the A rating category into the Aa and Baa categories. In 1968 there was a marked change into the A rating category from the Aaa and Aa categories.

The moderate deterioration indicated by the rating distributions of newly issued long-term state and local debt conforms with the previous conclusions from Table 23 on rated debt outstanding. The moderate deterioration indicated by both tables is noteworthy because it occurred despite the retirement of most of the low rated state and local bonds issued before the end of World War II.

Because of the substantial differences between general obligations and limited liability obligations and the increasing proportion of limited liability obligations newly issued and outstanding, it seems worthwhile to examine separate distributions for these two categories. There is no assurance that a particular rating will give the same indication of quality for a limited liability obligation as for a general obligation. Some observers feel the increasing proportion of limited liability obligations explains shifts in the total rating distributions. Other observers feel that although limited liability obligations are less safely secured than general obligations, the fact is not adequately recognized in the assigned ratings. Thus, deterioration may be occurring even if there are no major shifts in the total rating distributions.

Table 25 reveals the percentage distributions of rated general obligations. The rating distributions by dollar value outstanding indicate an improving trend in quality through the mid-1950's, leveling in the late-1950's, and moderate deterioration in quality from 1960 to 1966. The over-all level of quality of general obligations outstanding seems slightly higher in 1966 than it was in the 1940's. The percentage distributions based on the dollar value of general

TABLE 24

Percentage Distributions of Rated Long-Term State and Local
Bonds Issued, by Dollar Value in Year of Issue
(per cent in rating category)

Year	Aaa	AA	A	Baa	Ba & Below
By Dollar Value Including Public Housing Bonds					
1945	4.2	16.2	46.1	27.0	6.4
1946	7.6	22.7	47.6	19.2	2.8
1947	16.4	50.2	20.2	11.6	1.4
1948	33.9	23.2	31.2	10.5	1.1
1949	9.4	30.2	38.3	20.1	2.0
1950	12.6	41.2	32.6	12.0	1.5
1951	27.0	31.4	28.6	11.6	1.5
1952	23.5	21.2	42.5	10.6	2.1
1953	24.4	31.9	32.1	11.0	.6
1954	22.4	27.0	38.1	11.0	1.5
1955	22.2	29.6	35.0	12.2	1.0
1956	11.7	32.5	42.0	12.3	1.5
1957	11.3	38.2	38.9	11.0	.5
1958	16.4	36.1	35.0	10.8	1.7
1959	15.3	29.9	41.0	13.0	.9
1960	14.6	30.0	39.6	14.4	1.3
1961	12.5	36.4	37.4	12.8	.9
1962	17.3	22.6	45.6	13.2	1.3
1963	17.5	21.2	42.5	16.7	2.1
1964	13.2	28.2	41.6	15.5	1.5
1965	12.3	29.7	37.9	18.8	1.3
1966	10.0	32.5	32.2	24.1	1.3
1967	12.5	32.7	30.3	22.8	1.6
1968	8.7	27.9	40.3	22.1	.9
By Dollar Value Excluding Public Housing Bonds					
1951	15.0	36.5	33.2	13.4	1.8
1952	10.1	25.0	50.0	12.5	2.4
1953	13.0	36.7	36.9	12.7	.6
1954	13.3	30.2	42.6	12.3	1.6
1955	11.2	33.8	39.9	13.9	1.1
1956	7.2	34.1	44.1	13.0	1.6
1957	10.1	38.7	39.4	11.2	.5
1958	13.7	37.3	36.2	11.1	1.7
1959	10.2	31.7	43.4	13.7	1.0
1960	7.4	32.5	43.0	15.7	1.4
1961	9.1	37.8	38.9	13.3	.9
1962	12.4	23.9	48.3	14.0	1.4
1963	14.8	21.9	43.9	17.2	2.1
1964	5.9	30.5	45.1	16.8	1.7
1965	7.3	31.5	40.0	19.9	1.4
1966	5.0	34.3	34.0	25.4	1.3
1967	8.7	34.2	31.7	23.8	1.7
1968	5.0	29.1	41.9	23.0	1.0

Note: Rows may not add to 100 per cent because of rounding.

Source: Data from 1945-56 based on rating counts by NBER staff and data from 1957-68 from Investment Bankers Association.

TABLE 25

Percentage Distributions of Rated General Obligation Bonds
(per cent in rating category)

Year of Manual	Aaa	Aa	A	Baa	Ba & Below
Distributions by Dollar Value Outstanding					
1943	8.5	17.2	48.0	20.8	5.5
1949	11.9	17.0	55.8	11.6	3.7
1952	11.5	25.0	51.4	9.7	2.4
1954	13.8	30.5	44.7	9.4	1.6
1956	11.6	30.7	46.6	9.9	1.3
1958	11.5	27.7	49.2	10.6	1.0
1960	13.2	35.4	35.2	14.6	1.5
1966	9.4	30.9	39.9	18.1	1.6
Distributions by Number of Issuers					
1943	1.6	16.5	38.2	27.9	15.7
1948	5.3	24.0	38.2	23.5	9.1
1949	6.0	23.9	36.6	22.4	11.1
1950	6.1	24.3	37.9	22.7	8.9
1951	5.1	24.1	39.3	23.1	8.3
1952	4.8	22.9	39.2	23.9	9.1
1953	4.4	23.7	40.5	23.1	8.4
1954	4.3	22.9	40.7	26.0	5.9
1955	3.8	21.7	44.2	25.0	5.2
1956	3.3	21.2	46.7	24.5	4.3
1957	3.0	19.9	48.3	25.3	3.5
1958	3.2	20.2	47.7	26.1	2.8
1959	3.0	19.0	47.8	27.1	3.0
1960	2.7	17.2	46.6	30.1	3.4
1961	2.6	16.9	48.6	28.5	3.4
1962	2.7	15.9	49.2	29.2	2.8
1963	2.5	16.2	48.0	30.2	3.1
1964	2.6	14.6	49.9	30.3	2.7
1965	2.6	14.1	49.5	31.1	2.7
1966	2.6	15.0	48.6	30.9	2.9
1967	3.0	13.2	48.6	32.6	2.6
1968	3.0	12.3	49.4	32.9	2.1
1969	2.8	14.6	48.2	32.2	2.2

(continued)

TABLE 25 concluded

Year of Manual	Aaa	Aa	A	Baa	Ba & Below
		Distributions by Dollar Value Issued			
1957-58	14.7	37.3	36.2	10.9	.9
1959	13.8	36.9	35.6	12.4	1.2
1960	8.9	33.5	41.0	14.9	1.7
1961	11.2	39.2	36.0	12.5	1.1
1962	15.6	25.2	44.2	13.4	1.5
1963	13.0	26.6	43.8	14.9	1.6
1964	7.1	34.4	41.8	15.4	1.4
1965	9.1	33.0	37.8	18.7	1.4
1966	5.5	36.8	31.5	24.8	1.3
1967	10.7	38.0	30.2	18.9	2.2
1968	7.2	35.1	34.9	21.9	.9
1957-68[a]	10.2	34.7	37.0	16.6	1.4
		Distributions by Number Issued			
1957-58	5.8	27.4	43.8	21.0	2.1
1959	6.1	25.5	42.0	24.1	2.4
1960	6.4	23.8	42.8	24.3	2.7
1961	4.0	23.2	44.9	25.1	2.8
1962	5.4	22.5	44.7	24.7	2.7
1963	4.5	22.4	43.4	26.6	3.1
1964	3.8	22.0	44.0	27.3	3.0
1965	4.2	20.6	43.8	28.0	3.4
1966	4.3	23.2	42.8	26.9	2.8
1967	4.3	21.8	42.8	28.7	2.4
1968	3.4	20.1	45.2	28.8	2.5
1957-68[a]	4.8	23.2	43.7	25.6	2.7

Note: Public Housing Authority bonds are not included. Rows may not add up to 100.0 per cent because of rounding.

Sources: Data from Moody's Investors Service and the Investment Bankers Association.

[a]The figures in these rows are totals or percentages of totals for the period listed.

obligations newly issued help demonstrate why the rating distributions for the dollar value of outstanding general obligations indicated that the quality was strengthened in the 1950's, then weakened in the 1960's. The percentage distributions by dollar value issued from 1957 through 1968 usually indicated quality above that of outstanding issues in the early postwar years and below that of issues outstanding in 1958 and 1960.

The percentage distributions for the number of issuers with rated general obligations outstanding indicate that the quality of general obligations improved in the early postwar years but began deteriorating by the mid-1950's. A very moderate deteriorating trend appears evident since that time. The rating distributions for the number of newly issued general obligations also appear to indicate a moderate deteriorating trend in the quality of general obligations from 1957 through 1968. During this period, the proportionate number of newly issued general obligations that were rated Aaa or Aa declined slowly and the proportion that were rated Baa or Ba and below increased slowly.

Table 26 shows the percentage distributions of rated limited liability obligations. An examination of these distributions reveals that the proportions in most rating categories has fluctuated considerably during the postwar period. The largest fluctuation occurred between the rating distributions by dollar value outstanding for 1956 and 1958. Between those two dates, several large limited liability obligations were changed from the Aaa to the Aa rating category. Examination of the rating distributions by dollar value outstanding indicates that the quality of outstanding rated limited liability obligations increased until the mid-1950's and has weakened consistently since that time. The quality of outstanding rated limited liability obligations seemed roughly the same in 1966 as it was in 1949.

The rating distributions for the number of issuers of outstanding rated limited liability obligations also indicate an improvement in quality in the early postwar years, but a moderate deterioration since the mid-1950's. These distributions show that the percentage of limited liability obligations rated Aaa or Aa is lower and the percentage rate Baa or below is higher in the mid-1960's than in the immediate postwar period. The distributions by number of limited liability obligations issued show that the quality of newly issued limited liability obligations appeared to weaken slightly from 1957 through 1968.

Summary

When combined, all of the rating distributions analyzed indicate three moderate but distinct trends in the rating agency's evaluations of the postwar quality of rated long-term state and local debt. First, the quality of rated state and local bonds improved from the end of World War II into the early

TABLE 26

Percentage Distributions of Rated Limited Liability Obligations
(per cent in rating category)

Year of Manual	Aaa	Aa	A	Baa	Ba & Below
Distributions by Dollar Value Outstanding					
1943	.4	13.1	57.2	28.8	.5
1949	3.4	19.4	46.6	21.6	9.1
1952	.8	32.2	36.4	27.2	3.4
1954	1.0	30.1	47.5	16.4	5.0
1956	12.1	21.4	49.0	13.2	4.3
1958	2.9	31.7	46.2	15.5	3.7
1960	7.5	27.2	40.3	21.8	3.3
1966	5.8	19.4	44.9	22.8	7.1
Distributions by Number of Issuers					
1943	1.9	15.8	36.1	42.4	3.8
1948	.0	14.2	44.3	34.0	7.5
1949	2.0	17.5	40.0	33.5	7.0
1950	1.8	19.4	40.5	30.8	7.5
1951	1.6	28.3	39.5	24.5	6.1
1952	1.4	21.2	41.6	30.6	5.2
1953	.8	27.5	39.2	28.8	3.7
1954	1.4	25.4	40.8	28.6	3.6
1955	.7	21.0	47.3	27.3	3.7
1956	2.1	19.4	45.9	29.9	2.7
1957	1.8	18.2	43.9	33.6	2.6
1958	.8	20.0	45.9	29.7	3.6
1959	.7	16.7	44.6	34.6	3.4
1960	.9	14.3	43.2	37.9	3.7
1961	1.4	17.2	43.7	33.9	3.8
1962	1.8	13.2	45.4	35.4	4.2
1963	1.3	12.9	43.2	38.6	4.0
1964	4.0	10.7	44.6	36.3	4.4
1965	4.5	12.8	42.8	35.7	4.3
1966	4.7	10.9	43.0	38.1	3.4
1967	5.7	13.0	40.6	37.0	3.8
1968	5.2	12.6	43.3	35.5	3.5
1969	4.5	12.1	42.4	37.6	3.4

(continued)

TABLE 26 concluded

Year of Manual	Aaa	Aa	A	Baa	Ba & Below
		Distributions by Dollar Value Issued			
1957-58	.8	41.0	43.5	12.4	2.4
1959	.7	17.5	64.3	17.3	.3
1960	2.0	28.7	50.4	18.6	.3
1961	.5	32.1	50.7	16.5	.2
1962	7.3	18.1	58.9	15.0	.8
1963	17.6	13.0	44.3	21.9	3.3
1964	3.0	19.8	54.1	20.9	2.2
1965	1.8	26.7	46.8	23.5	1.2
1966	3.8	27.3	40.7	27.1	1.1
1967	2.3	26.8	37.2	32.6	1.0
1968	1.2	18.1	54.6	25.0	1.0
1957-68[a]	3.9	23.5	49.0	22.3	1.4
		Distributions by Number Issued			
1957-58	1.3	23.2	49.1	25.1	1.3
1959	.9	17.4	49.5	31.2	.9
1960	.9	18.5	46.4	32.9	1.4
1961	1.6	21.0	45.7	30.5	1.2
1962	1.2	16.5	49.5	30.3	2.4
1963	2.4	10.5	42.6	40.0	4.7
1964	3.2	13.8	44.3	35.7	3.0
1965	1.5	12.6	45.9	37.0	3.0
1966	2.6	18.8	39.9	35.7	2.9
1967	1.1	21.0	40.0	36.1	1.8
1968	1.9	13.7	50.3	32.1	2.1
1957-68[a]	1.8	16.5	45.6	33.7	2.4

Note: Rows may not add up to 100 per cent because of rounding.

Sources: Data from Moody's Investors Service and the Investment Bankers Association.

[a]The figures in these rows are totals or percentages of totals for the period listed.

1950's. Second, the quality of rated bonds remained relatively stable during the 1950's. Third, their quality has deteriorated moderately during the early and mid-1960's. The net effect of these postwar shifts in rating agencys' evaluations is that the quality of long-term state and local debt was roughly the same in the mid-1960's as it was in the years immediately following World War II.

Since rating agencies looked at roughly the same instrument and borrower characteristics examined in this study and at the future external environment, the preceding conclusion would seem to indicate that rating agencies felt the weakening in instrument and borrower characteristics was approximately overcome by an improvement in the future environment in which state and local debt will exist. The primary factor leading to this external improvement is the rating agency's assessment of a decrease in the probability of a serious economic decline.

8

QUALITY AS INDICATED BY MARKET YIELD RELATIONSHIPS

The money and capital markets' evaluation of instrument and borrower characteristics and of the external environment is another method that can be used to measure the quality of state and local debt. Relationships between market yields on various debt instruments are used to assess the money and capital markets' evaluation. This method of measuring the quality of state and local debt is very difficult to interpret because of the large number of factors, in addition to credit quality, that affect market yield relationships.

In this chapter, the use of market yield relationships as a measure of credit quality is briefly examined. Two categories of yield relationships are analyzed: (1) the relationships between yield indexes of federal government debt and state and local debt and (2) the relationships among the yields on different rating classes and different other classifications of state and local debt.

The Use of Market Yield Relationships as a Measure of Credit Quality

There are numerous explanations of the determinants of relative prices and, therefore, relative market yields among debt instruments.[1] In order to avoid a lengthy discussion of these explanations, which seems inappropriate for this paper, the author has divided what he believes are the primary determinants of market yield relationships among debt instruments into three broad groupings: supply factors, institutional factors and factors affecting the preferences of investors and potential investors among debt instruments. Factors affecting

---

[1]Several National Bureau publications (such as *The Cyclical Behavior of the Term Structure of Interest Rates* by Reuben A. Kessel and *The Behavior of Interest Rates* by Joseph W. Conard) as well as numerous other books and journal articles are devoted to various explanations of the determinants of market yield relationships.

propensities to save and consume and the choice between debt and equity type instruments are not treated as direct determinants of market yield relationships among debt instruments in this study.

The supply factors include the supply outstanding, the supply recently issued and the expected future supply among various types of debt instruments. In the author's opinion, these supply factors, tend to affect market yields because the various types of debt instruments compete as imperfect substitutes for investible funds at any point of time.[2] Figures on the amounts of various debt instruments outstanding and newly issued and short period predictions for coming debt issues are generally available.

Institutional factors often limit the investors' choice among debt instruments. Institutional practices and regulatory constraints tend to influence particular markets and limit arbitrage among markets, therefore, the market for debt instruments has a degree of segmentation rather than perfect homogeneity. Particular attention should be paid to changes in institutional practices and regulatory constraints since they may have an appreciable effect on market yields.

The debt investment preferences of owners of investible dollars also affect the market yields of debt instruments. The principal factors that seem to affect the preferences of investors and potential investors among debt instruments (i.e., the price they are willing to pay) are: (1) special terms in the debt contract, such as callability or convertibility; (2) the taxability of the return of the debt instrument; (3) the time of repayment; (4) the marketability of the debt instrument; and (5) the quality of the debt instrument.

Most of the effects of special terms and taxability can be removed as factors affecting the market yield by observing groups of debt instruments that are fairly homogenous in those areas. Where comparisons are made between the market yields on federal government securities (whose interest is now fully subject to income taxes) and the market yields on state and local indebtedness (whose interest is exempt from both personal and corporate income taxes at the present time), the observations are generally for short periods of time and major changes in both the personal and corporate income tax rate structures are separately taken into account.

The third factor affecting investment preferences, the time of repayment, can be caused by differences in maturity dates or in the way repayment is distributed over time. Two market characteristics, the increased doubt about the quality of an issue as the maturity lengthens and the lower interest rate risk as the maturity becomes shorter, explain much of the disparity between market yields due to this factor. For short-term issues with quality character-

---

[2]Some economists reject the notion that relative supplies of debt instruments materially affect their prices. In previous work the author has found high simple correlation coefficients between the relative supplies of state and local debt and federal government debt and the market yield differentials between these two types of debt instruments.

istics similar to those on long-term contracts, the lender generally feels more assured about the repayment of his debt instrument and believes its price will be more stable. Lenders with liquidity requirements are willing to pay a premium for these advantages unless there are unusual interest rate expectations or an unusual supply-demand situation for liquidity. In this study, most of the variations among market yields due to maturity or repayment differences are removed by considering only securities within given maturity and repayment groupings.[3]

Differences in the degree of marketability also affect the yield differential between debt instruments. Marketability is defined as the ability to sell a debt instrument within a very short time without obliging either the seller or buyer to make an appreciable concession from the price at which the debt instrument was last sold. Some investors, realizing that they may want or may be forced to buy or sell their debt instruments quickly, prefer a highly marketable issue and are willing to pay more, i.e., accept a lower yield, for this characteristic. Because of this added demand, market yields on debt instruments tend to be lower with increasing degrees of marketability.

Accurate information on measures that might indicate marketability, as the number of issues traded in a given time period or the spread between bid and asked prices, is generally not available at the present time. The size of the issue may be another indicator of the marketability of state and local debt. However, two studies by the Investment Bankers Association indicated that within homogenous rating groups there was no tendency for larger municipal issues to have a net interest cost advantage over smaller municipal issues. These studies suggest that, where the quality of the state and local issue is similar, small units do not suffer any significant disadvantage by selling their bonds in competition with large units.[4] Therefore, while the effects of marketability have not been removed, these effects seem relatively minor with the possible exception of some very small issues.

Differences in the quality of debt instruments are reflected in the market yields of debt instruments because lenders are willing to pay a higher price for a debt contract of a high quality borrower than for a similar contract of a lower quality borrower. Two interrelated reasons explain this preference. First, a more trustworthy borrower gives more complete assurance that the promised principal and interest will be paid. As the credit trustworthiness of the borrower declines, the lender becomes less certain the promised sums will be paid. Second, the maximum amount all borrowers, regardless of credit

---

[3]There are several other theories explaining the term structure of interest rates. The important point is that, no matter which theory is correct, the effects of the time of repayment are removed by comparing securities within given maturity and repayment groupings.

[4]*I.B.A. Statistical Bulletins* Nos. 3 and 5, Investment Bankers Association, Washington, D. C.

rating, will pay is the promised principal and interest. Thus, the promised sums are the most the lender can expect; all the possible variations from the promised sums are negative ones. The second reason clearly indicates that the mean values of the probable outcomes for the borrower with weaker credit are less than those for the sound borrower. Combined, these two reasons may be expected to induce the lender to lend to the less sound borrower only if he is offered better terms. The premium the lender demands from the weaker borrower should be determined by the prospective risk of default so that the amounts finally realized from large groups of debt instruments at several levels of quality should be approximately the same.

After adjusting for the effects of the discussed factors other than quality, market yield relationships have still been an imprecise measure of quality. For example, Hickman's study on the quality of corporate bonds from 1900 to 1943 pointed out that, after all defaults and redemptions were considered, the group of bonds with the lowest promised yield to maturity had a realized yield of 5.1 per cent and the group of bonds with the highest promised yield to maturity had a realized yield of 8.6 per cent.[5] Assuming similar terms, and assuming that the maturity dates and repayment schedules are comparable, the results following the earlier explanation should have been similar realized yields, i.e., the different promised yields should have been about equalized by the incidence of defaults.

Such differences in the results probably are primarily caused by the effects of market imperfections and uncertainty on market yield relationships. The competition among investors for debt instruments is far from perfect. For example, investors are often limited by regulations and a lack of knowledge or resources. Such limitations may distort the demand for some types of quality levels of debt instruments. Furthermore, while uncertainty, which takes the character of subjective probability distributions, exists in all debt instruments having any degree of credit risk, such uncertainty is usually highest for bonds with the highest promised yields. This uncertainty is indicated by the greater dispersion of the probable outcomes for borrowers with weaker credit. The premium for accepting such uncertainty may well account for a substantial part of the differences between realized yields.

Despite market imperfections and uncertainty, market yield relationships on state and local debt still appear to be a measure of credit quality that should be examined. Market yield relationships have been useful indicators of the credit ranking of many debt instruments despite their admitted weaknesses in quantifying the exact credit differences. For example, in the Hickman study the default rate was 5.9 per cent for corporate bonds with the lowest promised yield and continued, in sequential order, up to a default rate

---

[5]W. Braddock Hickman, *Corporate Bonds: Quality and Investment Performance,* Occasional Paper 59, New York, NBER, 1957. Hickman's study is the only available study of the long-run realized yield in any sector of the capital market.

of 42.4 per cent for corporate bonds with the highest promised yield.[6] Market yield relationships have been more effective as a measure of credit quality within one type or sector of debt instruments than among types or sectors.

Yield differentials are used in this study as an estimate of the money and capital markets' evaluation of the quality of state and local debt. Changes in yield differentials are traced to quality changes only after the potential effects of other explanatory factors are examined. It should be noted that quality may play a role even when other factors dominate. Two categories of yield differentials are examined. First, the relationships between the yields on state and local debt and federal government debt with similar maturities are used to indicate the absolute quality of state and local debt. Changes in the differential between these yields should represent meaningful changes in the yields on state and local debt, rather than changes in the level of all market yields. The yields on federal securities are used as the market yardstick since they are as free from credit risk as possible. An appreciable change in the differential between the yields on state and local debt and the yields on federal government debt should, *ceteris paribus,* indicate a change in the quality of state and local debt.

The relationships among the yields on state and local debt both in different rating classes and in different classifications are also studied. The yield differentials should indicate the money and capital markets' evaluation of quality and changes in quality among the various rating categories and classifications of state and local debt. They should also help indicate sectors of classifications where quality is or may become a problem.

Quality as Measured by Yield Relationships with Federal Government Bonds

The comparison of the long-term yields on state and local issues and federal government bonds should, *ceteris paribus,* indicate the money and capital markets' evaluation of the quality of state and local debt.[7] Since other things are seldom equal, the effects of major exogenous factors must be included in the analysis. For example, pronounced shifts in the annual rate of change of marketable federal debt outstanding, or in the annual rate of change of marketable state and local debt outstanding, may cause deviations from the usual relationship between yields on the two types of bonds. Changes in tax rates and the level of taxable income may also distort direct comparisons between the yield differential at various points of time.

---

[6]*Ibid.*

[7]Long-term yield index relationships should be the most meaningful measure of yield in state and local debt because most state and local debt outstanding is long-term and because the relative term structure of state and local debt has remained fairly constant.

The average quarterly yields on Moody's index of long-term, partially taxable federal bonds[8] and on the *Bond Buyer's* index of twenty tax exempt long-term general obligation bonds from 1921 through 1943 are presented in Chart 21. The *Bond Buyer's* index is the only current yield index that was available in the 1920's and early 1930's. The yield differential is found by subtracting the yield on state and local bonds from that on federal bonds at the same point of time. This yield differential appears in the lower section of Chart 21. When the effects of factors affecting market yields other than quality are removed or isolated, movement toward a larger negative yield differential should indicate the money and capital markets believed the quality of state and local debt deteriorated, while movement toward a positive yield differential should indicate the money and capital markets believed the quality of state and local debt improved. To obtain a more meaningful analysis, the lengthy period covered in Chart 21 is broken into four subperiods of shorter duration.

The movement toward a larger negative yield differential between partially taxable federal bonds and tax exempt state and local bonds in the subperiod from 1921 through 1925 indicates that the money and capital markets would not pay as much, i.e., demanded a higher yield premium, for state and local bonds relative to federal bonds. The primary factor leading to this movement was probably the pronounced decline in personal income taxes — the maximum tax rate fell from 58 to 25 per cent in this subperiod. Supply factors, such as the decline in the amount of marketable federal debt outstanding, also probably contributed to the widening of the negative yield differential during this period. Changes in the money and capital markets' evaluation of the quality of state and local indebtedness seem difficult to meaningfully isolate because of these other factors which also lead to an increase in the negative yield differential.

The negative yield differential between state and local bonds and partially taxable federal bonds became slightly wider during most of the second subperiod, 1926-31. During these years, the supply of marketable federal debt decreased at approximately a 5 per cent compounded rate, while the supply of state and local debt increased at approximately a 6 per cent compounded rate. These changes tend to have a widening influence on the negative yield differential. Personal and corporate income tax rates were constant during most of this subperiod; however, the short-term narrowing in the negative yield differential in late 1931 appears to be due to a large increase in personal income tax rates at that time. The maximum personal income tax rate went from 25 per cent in 1931 to 63 per cent in 1932. Once again the market yields were not sufficiently free of the affects of other factors to isolate the

[8]All of the interest on these bonds was exempt from the normal income tax, but only the interest on the first $5,000 of principal was exempt from the surtax. Most of the federal government bonds issued prior to March 1, 1941, were taxed in this manner.

CHART 21
Yield Relationship between U.S. Government Bonds and State and Local Bonds, Quarterly Yields, 1921-43

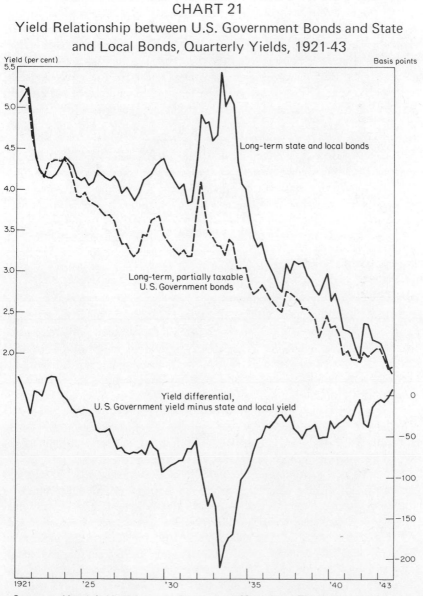

Sources: *Moody's Municipal and Government Manual* and *The Weekly Bond Buyer.*

money and capital markets' evaluation of changes in the quality of state and local debt.

In the third subperiod, 1932-34, the negative yield differential between federal bonds and state and local bonds widened substantially. The primary cause for this increase in the differential was clearly that the money and capital markets believed the quality of state and local debt had deteriorated. This deterioration is substantiated by the very large relative increase in the negative yield differential, in spite of other factors such as higher personal income tax rates and an increase in the amount of marketable federal debt outstanding while state and local debt outstanding remained fairly constant, which should have had a narrowing influence. By early 1935 the yield differential had returned to the 1931 level.

From 1935 through 1943, the last subperiod covered in Chart 21, the negative yield differential gradually became smaller and was positive in 1943. The factors contributing to this gradual narrowing include: an appreciable increase in the amount of marketable federal debt outstanding, a constant amount of marketable state and local debt outstanding, a steady increase in corporate income tax rates (from 13.75 per cent maximum to 40 per cent maximum in this subperiod), and an increase in personal income tax rates. Because of the effects of these factors, it seems unreasonable to make a conclusion about the changes, if any, in the money and capital markets' evaluation of quality for this subperiod.

In summary, the yield differential between long-term yields on state and local indebtedness and on federal bonds indicated significant positive or negative shifts in the quality of state and local debt in only one of the four subperiods covered in Chart 21, 1932-34. Changes in the yield differential between state and local bonds and government bonds in the other years covered by Chart 21 were not sufficiently free of changes in supply factors or changes in income tax rates to allow a definitive conclusion about quality. It is noticeable that both the decline and subsequent improvement in the money and capital markets' evaluation of the quality of state and local debt lagged behind the increase and decrease in defaults in the early 1930's.

Chart 22 is a continuation of Chart 21 from 1942 through 1968 except for one major change. The quarterly average yield on Moody's index of long-term, *taxable* federal bonds is compared with the quarterly average yield on long-term state and local issues because the interest on all federal bonds issued after 1941 was fully taxable. Because of the different yield index used for the federal bonds, they typically sold at higher yields than the tax-exempt state and local bonds. This change means that, *ceteris paribus,* significant narrowing of the positive yield differential (movement toward a negative differential) should indicate a decline in the money and capital markets' evaluation of state and local debt, while significant movement toward a larger positive yield differential should indicate an improved market evaluation.

In the period from 1942 through 1945 both personal and corporate in-

CHART 22
Yield Relationship between U.S. Government Bonds and State and Local Bonds, Quarterly Yields, 1942-68

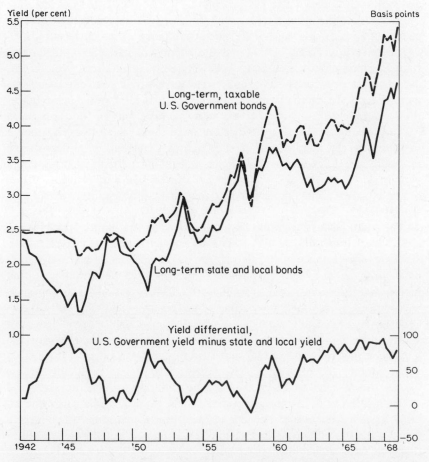

Yield (per cent)   Basis points

Long-term, taxable U. S. Government bonds

Long-term state and local bonds

Yield differential, U.S. Government yield minus state and local yield

Sources: Moody's Municipal and Government Manual and The Weekly Bond Buyer.

come tax rates rose, the amount of marketable U. S. government debt out-standing increased approximately fourfold and the amount of marketable state and local debt outstanding declined at a rate of approximately 5 per cent a year. These exogenous factors probably explain most of the increase in the positive yield differential during this period. The exact opposite of these factors — a decline in personal income tax rates, a decline in the amount of marketable federal debt oustanding and large increases in the amount of marketable state and local debt outstanding — probably explain most of the decrease in the yield differential in the four years following World War II.

Because of the marked changes in the above factors, no definitive conclusions can be made from market yields about changes in the money and capital markets' evaluation of the quality of state and local debt during World War II and in the years immediately following it.

Analysis of the period from 1949 through 1960 is simplified because personal and corporate income tax rates were fairly stable (there were small adjustments in 1951 and 1954) and the supply of marketable outstanding state and local debt increased at a relatively constant rate each year. In this period the shifts in the yield differential were relatively small and followed a definite cyclical pattern. The yield differential tended to widen in periods of prosperity and narrow during recessionary periods. Part of the explanation for this cyclical pattern may be that the money and capital markets believed there was a slight deterioration in the quality of state and local debt during recessionary periods and a slight improvement in its quality during boom periods. Much of the shifts in the yield differential from 1949 to 1961, however, seems to be explained by changes in the supply of marketable federal debt.[9]

The wider positive yield differential between federal bonds and state and local bonds from 1961 through 1965 calls for special attention. During several earlier periods covered in Chart 22 this yield differential had widened as much or more than it did from 1961 through 1965. During these earlier periods one or more of the other factors affecting market yields appear to have explained much of the widening in the positive yield differential. From 1961 through 1965, the supply of outstanding marketable federal debt grew slowly and at a constant rate; the supply of outstanding marketable state and local debt grew rapidly at a rate similar to its growth throughout the 1950's; and corporate and personal income tax rates were reduced slightly. These factors should tend to exert a narrowing influence on the positive yield differential between the two types of bonds. However, this narrowing influence was moderated by a change in institutional conditions – commercial banks were allowed to pay higher rates to attract certificates of deposits – that exerted a widening influence on the positive yield differential between federal bonds and state and local bonds in the 1961-65 period. Examined in the light of these changes in other factors the market yields in Chart 22 seem to indicate that the money and capital markets believed the quality of state and local debt remained constant or improved slightly from 1961 through 1965.

The yield differential was subject to conflicting influences – rapid growth in outstanding marketable federal debt, a 10 per cent surcharge on corporate and personal income taxes in 1968, and an even higher maximum rate on

[9]The Investment Bankers Association concluded that the rate of change in outstanding marketable U. S. government debt accounted for about half of the deviation from the normal yield relationship from 1954 through 1960. (*I.B.A. Statistical Bulletin,* November 1960, pp. 1-3).

commercial bank certificates of deposits – again from 1966 through 1968. Yield differentials changed little from their 1965 levels throughout the 1966-68 period, which may indicate that the money and capital markets believed the quality of state and local debt remained relatively stable.

Conclusions based on the relationship between the yields on long-term federal bonds and those on the *Bond Buyer's* index of twenty long-term state and local bonds might overlook changes in the quality of state and local bonds not covered by this index. The *Bond Buyer's* index is based upon three Aaa general obligations, eight Aa general obligations, eight A general obligations and one Baa general obligation. Conclusions about changes in quality from Chart 22, therefore, are based primarily on the yield relationships between federal bonds and Aaa and A general obligations. Large changes in the quality of Aaa or Baa general obligations or other types of state and local debt might be indicated by the yield relationships between these rating classes or types of state and local debt, and federal bonds, and not be observable in Chart 22.

Chart 23 depicts the yield differentials between the quarterly yields on Moody's index of long-term, taxable federal bonds and Moody's quarterly average yields for long-term Aaa and Baa general obligation bonds from 1942 through 1968. Since the two state and local yield averages are subtracted from the yield on federal bonds at the same point of time a significant positive increase in either or both of these yield differentials should, *ceteris paribus,* indicate an improvement in the quality of that rating class of general obligations. Similarly, a significant decrease in the positive yield differential should, *ceteris paribus,* indicate that the money and capital markets believed there was a deterioration in the quality of that rating class.

Analysis of Chart 23 indicates that both yield differentials had an upward trend from 1942 through 1945, a downward trend from 1945 through 1949, then followed a cyclical pattern from 1949 through 1960. The difference between the two yield differentials ranged from 70 to 120 basis points from 1942 through 1960. Thus, the yield differentials between federal bonds and both Aaa and Baa general obligations followed a pattern similar to the differential between the yields on federal bonds and those on the *Bond Buyer's* index of twenty state and local bonds from 1942 through 1960.

The 1960's are a different story. Yields on federal bonds exceeded yields on Baa general obligations in the early 1960's and exceeded these yields by roughly 50 basis points in the mid-1960's. During the same period yields on bonds did not rise over 100 basis points (as they did in the two earlier periods that federal yields exceeded Baa general obligation yields) above Aaa general obligations until the mid-1960's.

The money and capital markets appear to believe that the quality of Aaa general obligations remained fairly constant in the 1960's. This conclusion seems appropriate from 1961 through 1965 because the low rate of increase in the supply of outstanding federal debt and the small income tax reductions

CHART 23

Yield Differentials between U.S. Government Bonds and Aaa and Baa General Obligations, Quarterly Yields, 1942-68

```
·············· Baa general obligations minus Aaa general obligations
────── U.S. Government bonds minus Aaa general obligations
── ── ── U.S. Government bonds minus Baa general obligations
```

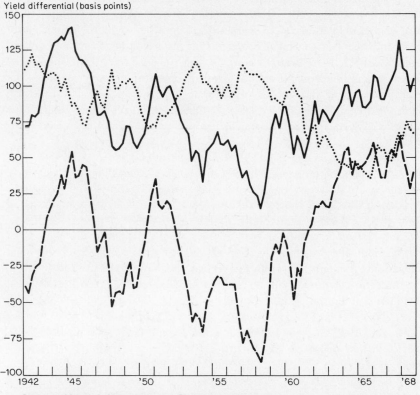

Source: Moody's Municipal and Government Manual.

in 1963 and 1964 probably slowed the widening of the yield differential. The moderate increase in this yield differential in the 1966-68 period seems explained more by the switch to rapid growth in marketable federal debt outstanding than by a change in the money and capital markets' evaluation of quality.

In the case of Baa general obligations, however, the money and capital markets seem to believe that the quality of debt in this rating category improved slightly in the early 1960's. Some of the widening in the positive yield differential was probably because commercial banks reached for higher yields in order to be able to attract certificates of deposits. On the other hand, the low rate of increase in federal debt and the income tax reduction in

1963 and 1964 should have had a narrowing influence. By the mid-1960's the widening slowed and the quality of Baa general obligations as indicated by market yields appeared to be relatively constant.

Quality as Measured by Yield Relationships between Different
Rating Categories and Different Types of State and Local Debt

Shifts in the relationship between the yields on federal bonds and the yields on an index of rated state and local general obligations with similar maturities provide only one way of measuring changes in the money and capital markets' evaluation of the quality of state and local debt. It seems equally important to study the level and any shifts in the relationships between the yields on state and local issues in different rating categories and between the yields on different types of state and local isssues. Such an analysis takes into account many issues not covered in the indexes of general obligations used so far and should indicate any appreciable changes in the money and capital markets' evaluation of the relative quality among various rating classes and types of such indebtedness. These yield comparisons should indicate the marginal classes of state and local debt, where the money and capital markets believe that the quality of the debt is materially different or has changed markedly from the quality indicated by the indexes used in the preceding section.[10] Since the analysis compares tax-exempt state and local yields, tax factors have little or no effect and changes in institutional conditions should have less of an impact.

Several types of yield relationships are examined. First, an analysis is made of the yield relationships among the various rating categories of general obligations. These relationships should help compare the evaluations of the money and capital markets as indicated by market yields with the evaluations of the rating agencies. The yields on unrated general obligations are then compared with the yields on rated general obligations. Since 49.5 per cent of the general obligations issued from 1957 through 1968 were not rated.[11] Some conception of the quality of unrated general obligations is necessary before reaching any over-all conclusions on the money and capital markets' evaluation of the quality of state and local debt.

[10]Some conclusions can still be made on the absolute quality of the different rating classes and types of state and local debt because the quality of Aaa general obligations was evaluated as being relatively constant in the postwar period and because the monthly yields on Aaa general obligations were highly correlated with the monthly yields on federal bonds for the mid-1956 through 1968 period.

[11]This proportion is based on the number of issues rated and unrated from the *I.B.A. Statistical Bulletins.* Figures from the same source show that these unrated bonds were 11.2 per cent of the total dollar amount of general obligations issued from 1957 through 1968.

The yields on rated and unrated state and local limited liability obligations are then compared with the yields on general obligations. This comparison should indicate areas where the money and capital markets feel the quality of limited liability obligations is substantially different, or has deteriorated or improved. In addition, the yield relationships between general obligations and rated limited liability obligations may give an impression of the comparability of the ratings given general obligations with the ratings assigned to limited liability obligations. Appendix Table 2 shows that limited liability obligations were nearly 40 per cent of the total amount of state and local debt outstanding in 1968, so a careful study of the money and capital markets' evaluation of the quality of limited liability obligations is very important to any over-all conclusions about the quality of such debt. Finally, the yields on special types of state and local debt, such as industrial aid bonds and toll road issues, are compared with the yields on rated obligations in order to isolate any special type or types of debt where the money and capital markets believe credit quality is materially different or has changed markedly.

The Yield Relationship Among
General Obligation Rating Categories

The yield differential between the long-term yields on Moody's indexes of Aaa general obligations and Baa general obligations was included in Chart 23 (page 136). These two indexes were chosen because they represent, respectively, the best and worst quality of rated general obligations for which yield computations are available. Narrowing of this yield differential should indicate an improvement in the quality of Baa general obligations relative to the quality of Aaa general obligations. Widening of this yield differential should indicate the converse.

Chart 23 shows that from the early 1940's through 1960 the yield differential between Baa and Aaa general obligations fluctuated in a narrow range from 70 to 120 points. There was no marked trend in the fluctuations within this range; however, the yield differential tended to widen slightly during recessionary periods and to narrow somewhat during boom periods. In this decade and a half of relatively mild economic fluctuations, the yields on Baa general obligations did not follow the countercyclical interest rate policies as closely as the yields on Aaa general obligations. The assumption is that in recessionary periods, when interest rates tend to be relatively low, a slight deterioration in the quality of Baa general obligations kept the yields on these obligations from falling as much as the yields on Aaa general obligations whose quality remained about the same. The opposite effect occurred in prosperous periods when interest rates were high. These offsetting effects of the slight changes in bond quality and countercyclical interest rate policies mean that during periods of mild economic fluctuations the prices of the lower rated Baa general obligations tend to fluctuate less than the prices of higher rated Aaa general obligations. Despite these small changes in the quality of Baa general obligations, the yield relationship between Baa and Aaa general obligations indicated the capital markets felt there was little in the way of substantial quality changes between these two rating categories from the early 1940's through 1960.

The only substantial postwar change in the money and capital markets' evaluation of the quality of Baa general obligations relative to Aaa general obligations, indicated by the market yields in Chart 23, began in 1961 when the yield differential broke through the postwar lower range limit of 70 basis points. From 1961 through 1965 the yield differential narrowed considerably indicating an improvement in the money and capital markets' evaluation of Baa relative to Aaa general obligations.[12] The narrowing trend in the yield differential appeared to end in 1966.

The improvement in the markets' evaluation of the quality of other rating categories of general obligations relative to Aaa general obligations is not limited to Baa general obligations. The yearly averages of the monthly differentials between the market yields of Aaa general obligations and those of Aa, A and Baa general obligations were:

	Aa minus Aaa	A minus Aaa	Baa minus Aaa
1957	22	65	105
1958	22	59	92
1959	14	50	81
1960	16	51	82
1961	14	34	61
1962	11	25	52
1963	8	20	43
1964	7	19	42
1965	7	19	40
1966	9	25	49
1967	10	26	55
1968	10	31	63[13]

Comparison of the decreases in these yield differentials shows that the yield differentials between Aaa general obligations and Aa and A general obligations have declined by at least as great a relative amount as the yield differential between Aaa and Baa general obligations. This decline in the yield differential seems to mean that the money and capital markets believed the

[12]As discussed earlier, the narrowing yield differential is also partly explained by commercial banks demanding more higher yielding state and local bonds to remain profitably competitive with higher maximum rates.

[13]Based on monthly new issue reoffering yields prepared by the Investment Bankers Association.

quality of both Aa and A general obligations also has improved slightly relative to the quality of Aaa general obligations from 1961 through 1965.[14]

Quality of Unrated Long-Term General Obligations

Up to this point the information on the quality of state and local debt as
indicated by market yield differentials has only taken into account the quality of rated long-term general obligations. In attempting to evaluate the over-
all quality of state and local debt this is a limited and biased sample.

Only 31,917 of the 76,277 state and local bonds recorded as issued from
1957 through 1968 were rated general obligations. Thus, rated general obligations comprised only 41.8 per cent of all state and local bonds recorded as
issued over this eleven year period. The dollar amount of long-term state and
local debt recorded as issued from 1957 through 1968 was $119,638 million.
Of this total, $70,066 million or 58.6 per cent was rated long-term general
obligations.[15]

The market yields of rated general obligation bonds would be a valid
sample for the population of all state and local debt if the market yields of
these general obligations were representative of the market yields on all state
and local debt. This supposition can be challenged even before observing the
yield data. For example, bond analysts typically feel many state and local
limited liability obligations should, *ceteris paribus,* command a higher yield
than general obligations because of the limited resources backing them. Unrated general obligations should often have a higher yield than rated general
obligations because of the limited marketability of most of these bonds and
the fact that many poorer quality general obligations are not rated.

Rating agencies usually do not rate state and local issues (1) under a
certain size, (2) as a matter of policy, or (3) where information was inadequate.[16] In addition, the major rating agencies do not rate some state and
local issues that are in a weak credit position. There are some pressures for
the rating services not to rate general obligations which they would rate
below A. Some state and local units with weak credit positions appear to
purposely fail to give the rating agencies information required for a rating.
The issuing unit prefers no rating to a rating below A for fear of higher
interest costs resulting from a rating below A. Some investment bankers also
discourage ratings on issues they feel might receive a low rating. There is also
a possibility that state and local units with only a small amount of debt

[14]The decline in these yield differentials is probably also partially explained by an
increased demand for higher yielding state and local bonds by commercial banks under
competitive pressures because of the higher maximum rate on certificates of deposits.

[15]Figures are based on data from the Investment Bankers Association.

[16]Both Moody's Investors Service (in *Moody's Manual*) and Standard and Poor's
Corporation (in *Municipal Bond Selector*) give these reasons for not rating some state
and local issues.

CHART 24
Monthly Median Yields on Unrated General Obligations and Baa General Obligations, 1957-68

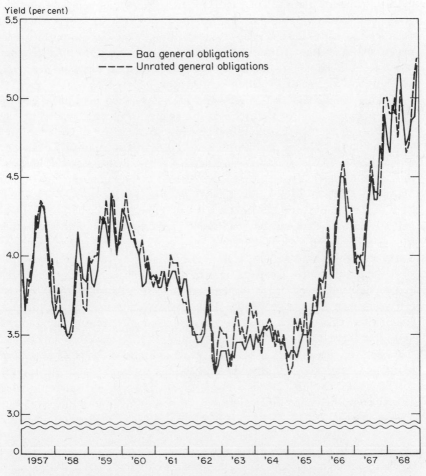

Yield (per cent)

Baa general obligations
Unrated general obligations

Source: Unpublished data from the Investment Bankers Association.

outstanding may be biased toward weaker credit position since they may have inexperienced financial management and lack diversification with respect to the resources used to support their indebtedness.

Chart 24 compares the monthly, median new issue reoffering yields on unrated and Baa general obligations from 1957 through 1968. This chart demonstrates that the median yield on unrated general obligations was close to that on Baa general obligations in most of the 144 months covered. The median yield on unrated general obligations exceeded the median yield on

Baa general obligations in seventy-nine months, was less than the Baa median yield in forty-eight months and was the same as the Baa median yield in seventeen months. Examination of the reoffering yields on individual issues used to compute the median yields revealed the average range of unrated general obligations (approximately 110 basis points or 1.1 per cent) was considerably wider than the average range of Baa general obligations (approximately 60 basis points) from 1957 through 1968. The cause of this wider range was unrated issues which had yields substantially in excess of the median yields on Baa general obligations.[17]

Analysis of the new issue reoffering yield information on unrated general obligations provides two insights into the quality of unrated general obligations. First, if the new issue reoffering yields are indicative of the quality of state and local debt, the quality of rated long-term general obligations is not representative of the quality of all general obligations. Instead, the addition of unrated general obligations tends to lower the average quality of all general obligations. Median yield figures indicate that the average quality of unrated general obligations was approximately the same as the quality of Baa general obligations. Individual new issue reoffering yields also indicated that the quality of some unrated general obligations was considerably below the quality of Baa general obligations with the highest yields.

Second, the median yields on unrated general obligations have tended to exceed the median yields on Baa general obligations more often in the last few years than in the late 1950's. This observation indicates that the new issue reoffering yields on unrated general obligations have not followed the narrowing trend relative to the yields on Aaa general obligations as much as the yields on Baa and other rated general obligations. Thus, if new issue reoffering yields are indicative of quality, the average quality of unrated general obligations has remained more stable relative to the quality of Aaa general obligations than other rated general obligations over the twelve years covered in Chart 24.

Quality of Limited Liability Obligations

Chart 25 compares the yield differentials between A, Baa and unrated limited liability obligations and similar general obligations from 1957 through 1968. The median new issue reoffering yields on the limited liability obligations exceeded the yields on the similarly rated general obligations in a narrow range of from 5-30 basis points in over three-fourths of the comparisons. Over the twelve year period, the yields on A limited liability obligations exceeded the yields on A general obligations by an average of 17 basis points. The yields on Baa limited liability obligations exceeded the yields on Baa

[17]The medians and ranges of new issue reoffering yields were compiled by the NBER staff from three sources: the Investment Bankers Association, Rand and Company and *The Weekly Bond Buyer.*

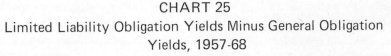

CHART 25

Limited Liability Obligation Yields Minus General Obligation
Yields, 1957-68

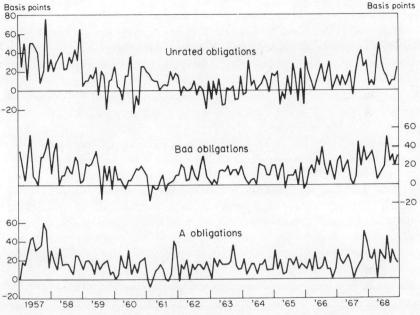

Source: Unpublished data from the Investment Bankers Association.

general obligations by an average of 14 basis points, and the yields on unrated limited liability obligations also exceeded the yields on unrated general obligations by an average of 14 basis points.[18]

The yield data in Chart 25 indicate that the money and capital markets have accepted fairly similar yields for limited liability obligations in similar rating categories. The monthly median yield in each rating category has averaged slightly higher for limited liability obligations than for general obligations. These yield relationships have remained remarkably stable over the twelve year period except in the case of unrated limited liability obligations. The median yield on unrated limited liability obligations exceeded the median yield on unrated general obligations by a monthly average of nearly 40 basis points in the late 1950's, but exceeded this general obligation median by an average of less than 5 basis points in the mid-1960's. There has been a trend, therefore, by the money and capital markets toward evaluating the

[18]There were not enough Aaa or Aa rated limited liability obligations to have meaningful monthly medians for the two categories. Individual Aaa or Aa limited liability issues generally had median reoffering yields which were slightly (0-20 basis points) above the similar Aaa or Aa general obligation median yields at the time of issue.

quality of unrated limited liability obligations as roughly equal to that of unrated general obligations. This observation seems particularly pertinent because between 40 and 50 per cent of the dollar amount and nearly three-fourths of the number of limited liability obligations issued from 1957 through 1968 were not rated.[19]

These yields relationships indicate that the money and capital markets evaluate the quality of limited liability obligations as being slightly below the over-all quality of general obligations. The quality of limited liability obligations in each rating category is slightly below the quality of general obligations in the same category. The quality of unrated limited liability obligations has improved to nearly equal to the quality of unrated general obligations.

Quality of Selected Special Classifications of State and Local Debt

Market yields offer one way to evaluate the quality of special classes of state and local debt. For instance, the market yields of state and local debt issued for a specific purpose or by a particular type of governmental unit can be compared with a state and local yield average. This yield comparison should indicate how the markets' evaluate the quality of the selected special class of state and local debt relative to the quality of the state and local debt represented by the yield average.

There is very little information currently available on the market yields of most classifications of state and local debt. Actual market yields are only available for a limited number of actively traded "dollar" bonds, and new issue reoffering yields have generally not been segregated into any special class groupings. All of the available yield information on two special classes of state and local debt in which quality has been questioned — the toll road bonds and the industrial aid bonds — is examined in the following paragraphs. The methods used should give some ideas about the procedures which can be followed and the problems which may arise as more yield information for special classifications of state and local debt becomes available.

Because of their competitive nature and limited liability, the quality of toll road bonds has often been questioned. Chart 26 compares the offering yields on toll road bonds issued from 1947 through 1955 with two yield indexes for the same period. Toll road bond offering yields show no clear pattern of conformity to the general market for state and local bonds; however, individual issues do appear to be influenced by this market. The offering yields on many of the toll road issues were substantially above the two yield indexes, indicating that the money and capital markets evaluated the quality of many toll road issues as being substantially below the quality of the state and local bonds represented by these two yield indexes.

---

[19]Based on figures obtained from the Investment Bankers Association.

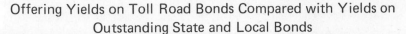

CHART 26
Offering Yields on Toll Road Bonds Compared with Yields on
Outstanding State and Local Bonds

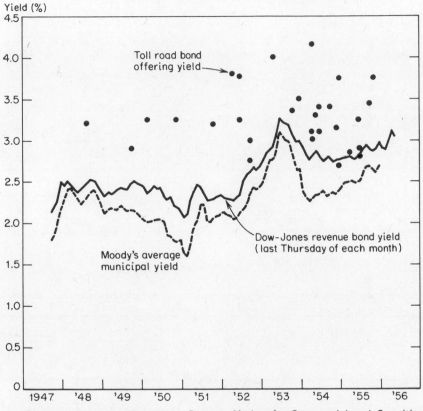

Source: Robinson, Roland I., *Postwar Market for State and Local Securities,* Princeton for NBER, 1960, p. 212.

The market yield information on the second selected special class of state and local debt, industrial aid bonds, is also limited. The twenty year new issue reoffering yields are available for only 85 of the 987 state and local industrial aid bonds reported to the Investment Bankers Association as issued between 1957 and 1968. The twenty year new issue reoffering yields on these industrial aid bonds are compared with the monthly median new issue reoffering yields on Baa general obligations from 1957 through 1968 in Chart 27. The yields on eleven of the eighty-five industrial aid bonds were below the monthly median yield on Baa general obligations. The reoffering yields on thirty-six of the eighty-five industrial aid bonds were from 0-50 basis points above the monthly median yield on Baa general obligations, while the yields on thirty-eight industrial aid bonds were over 50 basis points above the monthly

CHART 27
New Issue Reoffering Yields, 20 Year Maturity, for State and Local Bonds Issued for Industrial Aid, 1957-68

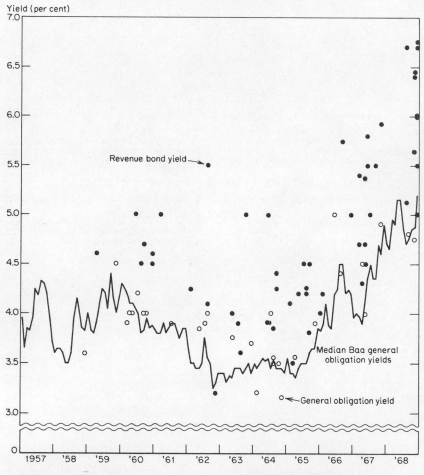

Source: Unpublished data from the Investment Bankers Association.

median yield on Baa general obligations. The yield information in Chart 27, therefore, indicates that the money and capital markets considered most industrial aid bonds to be of lower quality than the Baa general obligations. It also appears that the money and capital markets usually evaluated the quality of industrial aid revenue bonds as being weaker than the quality of general obligations issued for industrial aid.

Because of the limited size of this sample, all of the available net interest cost for industrial aid bonds issued from 1957 through 1968, with average maturities of from ten to twenty years, are examined. The net interest cost available for industrial aid bonds issued in these twelve years are:

Net Interest Cost	Industrial Aid Bonds		
	General Obligations	Revenue Bonds	Total All Bonds[20]
3.01-3.50	57	3	60
3.51-4.00	117	41	158
4.01-4.50	40	58	98
4.51-5.00	18	50	68
5.01-5.50	5	50	55
5.51-6.00	7	60	67
6.01-6.50	2	13	15
Above 6.50	0	4	4
	246	279	525

Net interest costs are not directly comparable with yields. However, despite some individual differences, the average net interest cost of the 85 industrial aid bonds for which market yields are available was approximately equal to the average of the net interest costs for the 525 bonds in the above tabulation. The above net interest cost information would, then, seem to agree with the earlier conclusions based on the limited number of available market yields. The majority of industrial aid bonds issued from 1957 through 1968 appear to be of weaker quality than Baa general obligations, with the quality of industrial aid revenue bonds evaluated as being weaker than the quality of general obligations issued for industrial aid.

The money and capital markets' evaluation of the quality of the two special classes of state and local debt discussed above is far from complete. As more yield information for these and other special classifications of state and local debt becomes available, market yields should become an important method of evaluating the quality of selected special classes of state and local debt.

Summary

To the extent that other factors affecting market yields can be eliminated, market yield relationships indicate the money and capital markets' evaluation of the quality of state and local debt. In this study, equal marketability is assumed; comparisons are made between yields on bonds with similar maturity dates and special terms; and the direction of the effects of changes in

[20]Data obtained from the Investment Bankers Association.

income tax rates, relative supplies and major institutional conditions are considered. There is no attempt, however, to measure the effect of these three changes.

Subject to this limitation, the relationships between the yields on state and local general obligations and the yields on U.S. government bonds (which as a class are as free from credit risk as possible) indicated:

1. The only time since 1921 during which the quality of state and local debt clearly showed a substantial change was from 1931-34 when quality deteriorated markedly.

2. From 1945 through 1961, when inferences on quality changes can be drawn they are in the expected direction, i.e., premiums fall in business expansions and rise in contractions. These changes occurred rapidly and were short lived; therefore, they may have been caused by changes in factors other than quality.

3. The quality of state and local debt remained constant or improved slightly from 1961 through 1965. Any over-all improvement was a result of an improvement in the quality of medium-grade rather than high-grade general obligations. The degree of effect of the increased rates commercial banks could pay on certificates of deposits is particularly difficult to ascertain in this period. From 1966 through 1968 quality appears to have remained relatively stable.

The relationship between yields in different rating categories and on different types and different classes of state and local debt indicates the money and capital markets' evaluation of the quality of one rating category, type or class relative to another. The primary other factor affecting these yield relationships is changes in institutional conditions. Because of the high correlation between yields on Aaa general obligations and yields on federal bonds, a reasonably accurate estimation of the money and capital markets' evaluation of the absolute quality of a rating category, type or class of state and local debt can be obtained through comparisons with the yields on Aaa general obligations. [21] The relationship between the yields on different rating categories, different types, and different classes of state and local debt indicated:

1. The quality of rated general obligations was ranked in accordance with the rating order — the quality of Aaa general obligations was the highest, with bond quality becoming lower as the rating became lower.

2. The only sizeable potential change in the quality of Baa general obligations relative to Aaa general obligations during the postwar period occurred in the 1961-65 period when the quality of Baa general obligations may have improved slightly relative to the quality of Aaa general obligations. The degree of the effect of the changes in the maximum rate banks that could pay on certificates of deposits is difficult to determine.

[21]The relationship between yields on Aaa general obligations and federal bonds is discussed in "The Postwar Quality of Municipal Bonds" by George H. Hempel, pp. 266-269.

3. The quality of Aa and A general obligations also may have improved slightly relative to the quality of Aaa general obligations in the 1961-65 period. Once again, the degree of the effect of the change in the maximum rate that banks could pay on certificates of deposits is difficult to determine.

4. The average quality of unrated general obligations was lower than the average quality of rated general obligations. Furthermore, there were wide dispersions in the quality of unrated general obligations; some issues were high quality, while others were very low quality.

5. The average quality of unrated general obligations is close to that of Baa general obligations. The quality of unrated general obligations appears to have declined slightly relative to the quality of Baa general obligations from 1957 to 1968.

6. The over-all quality of limited liability obligations has been slightly below the over-all quality of general obligations from 1957 through 1968 because: (1) the quality of limited liability obligations in each rating category has been slightly below the quality of general obligations in the same rating category; (2) the sizeable proportion of unrated limited liability obligations with an average quality roughly equal to that of unrated general obligations in recent years.

7. The quality of many toll road revenue bonds and many industrial aid bonds is substantially below the quality of Baa general obligations. The quality of industrial aid revenue bonds is generally below the quality of general obligations issued for industrial aid.

APPENDIX TABLE 1

Dollar Amount of State and Local Debt Issued, 1904-68
(millions of dollars)

| Year | Total Amount Issued | Short-Term Debt | | Long-Term Debt | | | |
		Public Housing Authority	Other	Total	Public Housing Authority	General Obligations[a]	Revenue Bonds
1968	25,033	2,062	6,597	16,374	528	9,084	6,763
1967	23,313	1,780	6,245	14,288	478	8,714	5,906
1966	17,612	1,740	4,784	11,089	440	6,573	4,076
1965	17,622	1,865	4,672	11,084	464	6,981	3,639
1964	15,967	1,892	3,531	10,544	636	6,250	3,658
1963	15,587	1,961	3,520	10,107	254	5,815	4,037
1962	13,322	1,727	3,036	8,558	382	5,510	2,666
1961	12,874	1,469	3,044	8,360	189	5,573	2,598
1960	11,236	1,283	2,723	7,230	383	4,652	2,195
1959	11,860	1,563	2,616	7,681	310	4,850	2,521
1958	11,359	1,675	2,235	7,449	182	5,543	1,724
1957	10,232	1,599	1,675	6,958	65	4,868	2,025
1956	8,153	1,222	1,484	5,446	199	3,577	1,670
1955	8,569	1,327	1,266	5,977	474	3,771	1,732
1954	10,319	1,897	1,453	6,969	374	3,381	3,214
1953	8,315	1,679	1,078	5,558	496	3,495	1,567
1952	6,450	955	1,094	4,401	304	2,634	1,463
1951	4,915	540	1,097	3,278	328	2,220	730
1950	5,305	544	1,067	3,694	59	3,035	600
1949	4,328	370	963	2,995	143	2,169	683
1948	3,994	307	698	2,990	66	2,374	550
1947	3,311	250	708	2,354	4	1,964	386
1946	1,944	252	489	1,204	19	980	205
1945	1,484	225	440	819	3	613	203
1944	1,281	252	317	712	13	457	242
1943	1,219	239	472	508	61	291	156
1942	1,689	425	688	576	89	390	97
1941	2,637	392	1,016	1,229	22	1,099	108
1940	3,124	495	1,131	1,498	22	1,288	188
1939	2,307	51	1,157	1,099	0	981	118
1938	2,397	0	1,168	1,229	0	1,078	151
1937	1,696	0	712	984	0	832	152
1936	1,889	0	733	1,156	0	1,039	117
1935	2,183	0	988	1,196	0	1,080	116
1934	2,108	0	933	1,175	0	1,159	16
1933	2,116	0	988	1,128	0	1,128	n
1932	2,029	0	1,092	937	0	937	n
1931	2,339	0	1,087	1,252	0	1,166	86
1930	2,335	0	952	1,383	0	1,369	14

(continued)

APPENDIX TABLE 1 concluded

Year	Total Amount Issued	Short-Term Debt			Long-Term Debt		
		Public Housing Authority	Other	Total	Public Housing Authority	General Obligations[a]	Revenue Bonds
1929	2,363	0	921	1,442	0	1,399	43
1928	2,107	0	717	1,390	0	1,370	20
1927	2,103	0	625	1,478	0	1,465	13
1926	2,023	0	661	1,362	0	1,317	45
1925	2,271	0	866	1,405	0	1,392	13
1924	2,426	0	979	1,447	0	1,440	7
1923	1,649	0	514	1,135	0	1,134	1
1922	1,675	0	396	1,280	0	1,277	3
1921	2,145	0	762	1,383	0	1,376	7
1920	1,438	0	664	774	0	773	1
1919	1,220	0	450	770	0	753	17
1918	736	0	473	263	0	263	n
1917	837	0	392	445	0	444	1
1916	790	0	292	497	0	495	2
1915	647	0	155	493	0	292	1
1914	732	0	286	446	0	446	n
1913	892	0	483	408	0	408	n
1912	591	0	192	399	0	399	n
1911	643	0	191	452	0	451	1
1910	522	0	197	324	0	324	n
1909	482	0	118	364	0	364	n
1908	530	0	175	355	0	355	n
1907	469	0	167	301	0	301	n
1906	426	0	125	301	0	301	n
1905	348	0	150	198	0	198	n
1904	417	0	131	287	0	287	n

Sources: Public housing debt figures obtained from the Public Housing Administration. Revenue bonds issued from 1904 through 1937 compiled by NBER staff from files at The Bond Buyer, Inc. and John F. Fowler, *Revenue Bonds,* New York, 1938. Other figures obtained from The Bond Buyer's *Municipal Finance Statistics,* Vol. IV, New York, 1969.

[a]General obligations in this appendix are total long-term debt less public housing bonds and revenue bond, and include nonguaranteed special assessment bonds, which are limited liability obligations.

n = Amount issued less than $500,000.

APPENDIX TABLE 2

Dollar Amount of State and Local Debt Outstanding, Selected Years from 1902 Through 1968
(millions of dollars)

		Short-Term Debt		Long-Term Debt			
Year[a]	Total Debt Outstanding	Public Housing Authority	Other	Total	Public Housing Authority	Other General Obligations[b]	Limited Liability Obligations[b]
1968[a]	121,158	1,117	7,310	112,731	5,297	59,781	47,653
1967[a]	114,614	976	6,017	107,621	4,845	57,917	44,859
1966[a]	107,051	979	5,072	101,000	4,537	55,263	41,200
1965[a]	99,512	911	4,398	94,204	4,224	52,194	37,786
1964[a]	92,222	1,001	3,694	87,527	3,804	49,462	34,261
1963	87,451	980	3,320	83,151	3,533	47,172	32,446
1962	81,278	977	2,758	77,543	3,270	45,051	29,222
1961	75,023	846	2,637	71,540	3,016	41,646	26,878
1960	69,955	731	2,423	66,801	2,872	38,778	25,151
1959	64,110	853	2,130	61,127	2,566	36,697	21,864
1958	58,187	816	1,635	55,737	2,383	33,461	19,893
1957	53,039	688	1,506	50,845	2,296	30,714	17,835
1956	48,868	720	1,373	46,775	2,181	29,634	14,960
1955	44,267	963	1,032	42,272	1,864	27,461	12,947
1954	38,931	1,203	830	36,898	1,407	25,586	9,905
1953	33,782	1,037	741	32,004	1,270	23,003	7,731
1952	30,100	849	531	28,720	857	21,579	6,284
1951	27,040	549	942	25,549	409	20,943	4,197
1950	24,115	239	821	23,056	414	19,378	3,264
1949	20,999	220	514	20,265	418	17,369	2,478
1948	18,656	223	360	18,073	414	15,739	1,920
1947	16,815	233	136	16,446	419	14,143	1,884
1946	15,917	232	23	15,662	423	13,241	1,998
1945	16,671	232	127	16,312	427	13,794	2,091
1944	17,479	244	381	16,854	434	14,238	2,182
1943	18,773	245	475	18,053	435	15,162	2,456
1942	19,337	299	632	18,406	338	15,482	2,586
1941	19,907	336	792	18,779	203	15,905	2,671
1940	20,283	287	948	19,048	33	16,347	2,668
1937	19,462	0	875	18,587	0	15,887	2,700
1932	19,205	0	1,331	17,874	0	15,869	2,005
1927	14,881	0	545	14,336	0	14,336[c]	
1922	10,109	0	654	9,455	0	8,661	794
1913	4,414	0	220	4,194	0	4,194[c]	
1902	2,107	0	100	2,007	0	2,007[c]	

Notes to Appendix Table 2

Note: Census data for *excluded* years prior to 1940 are not consistent with definition and data in this study.

Sources: Figures obtained from records of the Governments Division of U.S. Bureau of the Census and the Public Housing Administration.

[a]All data based on June 30 fiscal years starting in 1964. Prior to 1964 some local governments reported on different fiscal year bases. Total state and local debt outstanding was $85,056 in 1963 using the June 30 fiscal year basis for all local governments.

[b]Limited liability obligations were slightly understated and other general obligations overstated from 1948 to 1951 because some nonguaranteed special assessment bonds were (incorrectly) classified as general obligations. Prior to 1948 limited liability obligations were the total of revenue bonds and nonguaranteed special assessment bonds.

[c]Limited liability obligations were not separated from other long-term debt in 1927, 1913 and 1902.

APPENDIX TABLE 3

Dollar Amount of Long-Term State and Local Debt Outstanding, by Type of
Governmental Unit in Selected Years from 1902 Through 1968
(millions of dollars)

Year[a]	States	All Local	Counties	Incorporated Municipalities	Unincorporated Municipalities	School Districts	Special Districts[b]
1968[a]	33,622	79,109	8,462	33,942	1,973	18,016	16,716
1967[a]	31,185	76,436	7,685	32,186	1,950	18,006	16,611
1966[a]	28,504	72,497	6,841	30,892	1,723	17,368	15,664
1965[a]	26,235	67,969	6,367	29,280	1,707	16,290	14,325
1964[a]	24,401	63,126	5,818	27,773	1,651	15,257	12,627
1963	22,751	60,399	5,623	26,913	1,556	14,363	11,945
1962	21,561	55,982	5,247	24,866	1,315	13,767	10,787
1961	19,530	52,012	4,791	23,566	1,080	12,696	9,878
1960	18,128	48,673	4,900	21,900	1,035	11,800	9,000
1959	16,421	44,706	4,600	20,900	949	11,300	7,000
1958	15,065	40,672	4,100	19,400	1,000	10,000	6,200
1957	13,522	37,013	3,502	17,941	1,059	8,995	5,517
1956	12,643	34,424	3,343	16,140	956	8,394	5,593
1955	10,951	31,322	2,960	15,302	833	7,098	5,128
1954	9,317	27,581	2,624	13,893	782	5,827	4,454
1953	7,505	24,499	2,370	12,912	647	4,551	4,018
1952	6,640	22,081	1,937	12,113	604	3,715	3,710
1951	6,101	19,447	1,795	11,285	368	3,130	2,870
1950	5,254	17,887	1,629	10,577	308	2,590	2,784
1949	4,014	16,126	1,535	9,223	268	2,044	3,055
1948	3,716	14,357	1,370	8,641	247	1,477	2,621
1947	2,894	13,552	1,442	7,914	166	1,294	2,736
1946	2,333	13,334	1,381	7,981	155	1,220	2,597
1945	2,422	13,890	1,410	8,270	170	1,273	2,667
1944	2,760	14,086	1,659	8,407	191	1,380	2,449
1943	2,856	14,916	1,580	9,067	254	1,495	2,520
1942	3,067	15,657	1,776	9,485	250	1,626	2,520
1941	3,171	15,841	1,943	9,555	260	1,669	2,414
1940	3,280	16,057	2,036	9,511	280	1,699	2,531
1937	3,073	15,393	2,238	9,175	310	1,724	1,946
1932	2,502	15,317	2,548	9,157	343	1,987	1,282
1922	1,106	8,474	1,282	5,477	101	985	627
1913	423	4,075	393	3,447	80	119	36
1902	270	1,924	205	1,612	56	46	5

Note: Census data for *excluded* years prior to 1940 are not consistent with definition
and data in this study.

Source: Figures obtained from records of the Governments Division of U.S. Bureau of
the Census.

[a]All data based on June 30 fiscal years starting in 1964. Prior to 1964 some local
governments reported on different fiscal year bases.

[b]The classification special districts (other than school districts) includes some local
statutory authorities. State statutory authorities and the remaining local statutory authorities are included as nonguaranteed debt of the issuing governmental unit. A further
breakdown of these figures is not available at the present time.

APPENDIX TABLE 4

Net Debt Figures and Measures of Economic Activity in the United States, 1916-68
(billion of dollars)

Year	Net Total Public and Private Debt[a]	Net Public Debt[a]	Net State and Local Debt[a]	Net Stock of Total Wealth[b]	Net State and Local Wealth[b]	Gross National Product	National Income[c]	Disposable Personal Income
1968	1,568.5	441.9	128.6			860.6	712.8	589.0
1967	1,419.1	410.7	113.4			789.7	652.9	546.3
1966	1,331.7	388.6	102.7			747.6	620.8	511.6
1965	1,240.2	373.7	96.4			684.9	564.3	473.2
1964	1,151.8	363.3	89.3			632.4	518.1	438.1
1963	1,068.9	348.2	82.0			590.5	481.9	404.6
1962	995.6	336.1	75.7			560.3	457.7	385.3
1961	947.7	318.1	67.0			520.1	427.3	364.4
1960	890.2	304.0	61.0			503.7	414.5	350.0
1959	846.2	299.8	55.6			483.7	400.0	337.3
1958	782.6	283.6	50.9	1,702.8	190.6	447.3	367.8	318.8
1957	738.9	271.1	46.7	1,629.8	180.3	441.1	366.1	308.5
1956	707.5	268.1	42.7	1,518.1	167.7	419.2	350.8	293.2
1955	672.3	269.8	38.4	1,401.9	152.1	398.0	331.1	275.3
1954	612.0	263.6	33.4	1,306.3	138.8	364.8	303.1	257.4
1953	586.4	256.7	28.6	1,259.3	129.6	364.6	304.7	252.6
1952	555.2	248.7	25.8	1,214.1	123.3	345.5	291.4	238.3
1951	524.0	241.8	23.3	1,164.6	115.3	328.4	278.0	226.6
1950	490.3	239.4	20.7	1,067.1	106.2	284.8	241.1	206.9
1949	448.4	236.7	18.1	932.0	94.2	256.5	217.5	188.6
1948	433.6	232.7	16.2	928.4	95.9	257.6	224.2	189.1
1947	417.4	237.7	14.4	843.5	90.1	231.3	199.0	169.8
1946	397.4	243.3	13.6	700.9	76.4	208.5	181.9	160.0

APPENDIX TABLE 4 continued

Year	Net Total Public and Private Debt[a]	Net Public Debt[a]	Net State and Local Debt[a]	Net Stock of Total Wealth[b]	Net State and Local Wealth[b]	Gross National Product	National Income[c]	Disposable Personal Income
1945	406.3	266.4	13.7	576.2	61.7	212.0	181.5	150.2
1944	370.8	226.0	14.1	538.2	58.1	210.1	182.6	146.3
1943	313.6	169.3	14.9	522.9	57.0	191.6	170.3	133.5
1942	259.0	117.5	15.8	505.2	56.1	167.9	137.1	116.9
1941	211.6	72.6	16.3	473.1	53.9	124.5	104.2	92.7
1940	189.9	61.3	16.5	424.2	49.6	99.7	81.1	75.7
1939	183.2	58.9	16.3	395.6	47.5	90.5	72.6	70.3
1938	179.6	56.5	16.0	384.4	46.5	84.7	67.4	65.5
1937	182.0	55.3	16.1	383.4	46.8	90.4	73.6	71.2
1936	180.3	53.9	16.2	366.6	44.7	82.5	65.0	66.3
1935	174.7	50.5	16.0	344.9	42.4	72.2	57.2	58.5
1934	171.4	46.3	15.9	341.8	42.4	65.1	49.5	52.4
1933	168.5	41.0	16.7	330.2	40.8	55.6	40.3	45.5
1932	174.6	37.9	16.6	323.1	36.8	58.0	42.8	48.7
1931	181.9	34.0	15.5	360.1	37.7	75.8	59.7	64.0
1930	191.0	30.6	14.1	410.1	38.5	90.4	75.4	74.5
1929	190.9	29.7	13.2	439.1	38.1	103.1	86.8	83.3
1928	185.9	29.8	12.3	430.6	36.6	95.6	78.7	
1927	177.3	29.7	11.5	413.9	34.6	93.5	75.9	
1926	168.8	29.9	10.7	398.9	32.7	95.3	76.6	
1925	162.6	30.3	10.0	384.2	31.1	90.0	73.7	
1924	153.0	30.0	9.0	367.6	29.4	83.4	69.1	

APPENDIX TABLE 4 concluded

Year	Net Total Public and Private Debt[a]	Net Public Debt[a]	Net State and Local Debt[a]	Net Stock of Total Wealth[b]	Net State and Local Wealth[b]	Gross National Product	National Income[c]	Disposable Personal Income
1923	146.3	30.0	8.2	357.1	28.2	84.3	69.5	
1922	140.0	30.5	7.7	334.2	26.1	72.5	59.5	
1921	135.8	29.6	6.5	328.6	25.8	70.3	51.7	
1920	135.4	29.6	5.9	374.4	29.2	86.2	69.5	
1919	128.0	30.8	5.2	373.0	29.1	77.1	68.2	
1918	117.4	25.9	5.0	314.4	24.6	65.5	58.3	
1917	94.4	12.0	4.7	274.4	21.7	59.5	53.7	
1916	82.1	5.6	4.4	226.8	18.1	47.8	44.8	

[a]U.S. Department of Commerce, *Survey of Current Business*, May 1969, May 1966, May 1965 and July 1960 issues.

[b]1945-58 data from R. W. Goldsmith, *The National Wealth of the United States in the Postwar Period*, Princeton for NBER, 1962, p. 112, 1916-44 data from R. W. Goldsmith, U.S. Brady, and H. Mendershausen, *A Study of Savings in the United States*, Princeton, N.J., 1956, p. 14. While similar definitions and measurement techniques were used in both studies, these two series are not directly connectable.

[c]1929-65 data from U.S. Department of Commerce, *Survey of Current Business* May 1969, May 1966 and August 1965 issues. 1916-28 figures from estimates of Office of Business Economics, U.S. Department of Commerce (1916-58 figures are not directly comparable with figures after 1928).

SELECTED BIBLIOGRAPHY

Selected Bibliography

The following bibliography makes no attempt to be an exhaustive list of references related to the quality of state and local debt. Instead, it merely lists those books, articles, public documents, periodicals and other sources which were particularly helpful in writing this study.

Books

1. Adams, H.C. *Public Debt*. New York: D. Appleton-Century, 1890.

2. Atkinson, Thomas R. *Trends in Corporate Bond Quality*. Studies in Corporate Bond Financing No. 4. New York: National Bureau of Economic Research, 1967.

3. Badger, R.E. and Guthmann, H.G. *Investment Principles and Practices*. New York: Prentice-Hall, Inc., 1951.

4. Buchanan, James M. *Public Principles of Public Debt*. Homewood, Ill.: Richard D. Irwin, Inc., 1958.

5. Burkhead, Jesse. *Government Budgeting*. New York: John Wiley & Sons, Inc., 1959.

6. Burns, Arthur F. and Mitchell, Wesley C. *Measuring Business Cycles*. Studies in Business Cycles No. 2. New York: National Bureau of Economic Research, 1946.

7. Calvert, Gordon L. (ed.). *Fundamentals of Municipal Bonds.* Washington: Investment Bankers Association of America, 1965.

8. Chatters, Carl H. (ed.). *Municipal Debt Defaults: Their Prevention and Adjustment*. Chicago: Municipal Financial Officers Association, 1933.

9. Chatters, Carl H., and Hillhouse, Albert M. *Local Government Debt Administration*. New York: Prentice-Hall, Inc., 1939.

10. Conard, Joseph W. *The Behavior of Interest Rates: A Progress Report*. New York: National Bureau of Economic Research, 1966.

11. Cooke, Helen J. *The Role of Debt in the Economy*. Washington: Public Affairs Press, 1961.

12. Copeland, Morris A. *Trends in Government Financing*. Princeton: Princeton University Press for National Bureau of Economic Research, 1961.

13. Curwin, Winthrop S. *A Manual on Municipal Bonds*. New York: Smith, Barney & Co., 1956.

14. Davis, Edward H. *Of the People, By the People, For the People*. New York: John Nuveen & Co., 1958.

15. Due, John F. *Government Finance: An Economic Analysis*. Homewood, Ill.: Richard D. Irwin, Inc., 1959.

16. *Financing Metropolitan Government*. The Summary of a Symposium Conducted by the Tax Institute. Princeton: Tax Institute, Inc., 1955.

17. Fitch, Lyle C. *Taxing Municipal Bond Income*. Berkeley: University of California Press, 1950.

18. Friend, Irwin. *Investment Banking and the New Issues Market: Summary Volume*. Philadelphia: University of Pennsylvania, 1965.

19. Freund, William C., and Lee, Murray G. *Investments Fundamentals*. New York: American Bankers Association, 1966.

20. Fowler, John F. *Revenue Bonds*. New York: Harper & Brothers, Publishers, 1938.

21. Fuller, Donald R. *Government Financing of Private Enterprise*. Stanford: Stanford University Press, 1948.

22. Goldsmith, Raymond W. *The National Wealth of the United States in the Postwar Period*. Princeton: Princeton University Press for National Bureau of Economic Research, 1962.

23. Goldsmith, Raymond W., Brady, Dorothy S., and Menderhausen, Horst. *A Study of Savings in the United States*, Vol. III: Special Studies. Princeton: Princeton University Press, 1956.

24. Goldsmith, Raymond W., Lipsey, Robert E., and Mendelson, Morris. *Studies in the National Balance Sheet of the United States.: Vol. II. Studies in Capital Formation and Financing No. 11. Princeton:* Princeton University Press for National Bureau of Economic Research, 1963.

25. Goodbody & Company. *Industrial Aid Financing*. New York: Goodbody & Co., 1966.

26. Groves, Harold M. *Financing Government*. New York: Holt, Rinehart, and Winston, Inc., 1964.

27. Gurley, J.G., and Shaw, E.S. *Money in a Theory of Finance*. Washington: The Brookings Institution, 1960.

28. Harold, Gilbert. *Bond Ratings as an Investment Guide*. New York: The Ronald Press Co., 1938.

29. Hart, Albert G. (ed.). *Debts and Recovery 1929 to 1937*. New York: Twentieth Century Fund, Inc., 1938.

30. Heins, A. James. *Constitutional Restrictions Against State Debt*. Madison: University of Wisconsin Press, 1963.

31. Herber, Bernard P. *Modern Public Finance*. Homewood, Ill.: Richard D. Irwin, 1967.

32. Hempel, George H. "The Postwar Quality of Municipal Bonds" (unpublished dissertation). Ann Arbor: University of Michigan, 1964.

33. Hickman, W. Braddock. *Corporate Bonds: Quality and Investment Performance*. Occasional Paper No. 59. New York: National Bureau of Economic Research, 1957.

34. Hillhouse, Albert M. *Defaulted Municipal Bonds*. Chicago: Municipal Finance Officers' Association, 1935.

35. Hillhouse, Albert M. *Municipal Bonds: A Century of Experience*. New York: Prentice-Hall, Inc., 1936.

36. Homer, Sidney. *A History of Interest Rates*. New Brunswick, N.J.: Rutgers University Press, 1963.

37. Horton, Donald C. *Long-term Debts in the United States*. Sponsored by the U.S. Department of Commerce. Washington: Government Printing Office, 1937.

38. Kessel, Reuben A. *The Cyclical Behavior of the Term Structure of Interest Rates*. Occasional Paper No. 91. New York: National Bureau of Economic Research, 1965.

39. Klein, Philip A. and Moore, Geoffrey H. *The Quality of Consumer Instalment Credit*. Studies in Consumer Instalment Financing No. 13. New York: National Bureau of Economic Research, 1967.

40. Knappen, Laurence S. *Revenue Bonds and the Investor*. New York: Prentice-Hall, Inc., 1939.

41. Lent, George E. *The Ownership of Tax-Exempt Securities, 1913-1953*. Occasional Paper No. 47. New York: National Bureau of Economic Research, 1955.

42. McDiarmid, Fergus J. *Investing for a Financial Institution*. New York: Life Office Management Association, 1961.

43. Maxwell, James A. *Tax Credits and Intergovernmental Fiscal Relations*. Washington: The Brookings Institution, 1962.

44. Maxwell, James A. *Financing State and Local Governments*. Studies of Government Finance. Washington: The Brookings Institution, 1965.

45. Meiselman, David. *The Term Structure of Interest Rates*. Englewood Cliffs, N.J..: Prentice-Hall, Inc., 1962.

46. Mikesell, R.M. and Hay, Leon E. *Governmental Accounting*. Homewood, Ill.: Richard D. Irwin, 1969.

47. *Municipal Finance Administration*. Chicago: The International City Managers Association, 1962.

48. Musgrave, Richard A. *The Theory of Public Finance.* New York: McGraw-Hill Book Co., 1959.

49. *Public Finances: Needs, Sources, and Utilization.* Universities- National Bureau Conference Series 12. Princeton: Princeton University Press for National Bureau of Economic Research, 1961.

50. Ott, David J., and Meltzer, Allan H. *Federal Tax Treatment of State and Local Securities.* Washington: The Brookings Institution, 1963.

51. Ratchford, Benjamin U. *American State Debts.* Durham, N.C.: Duke University Press, 1941.

52. Raymond, William L. *State and Municipal Bonds.* New York: Financial Publishing Co., 1932.

53. Robinson, Roland I. *Postwar Market for State and Local Government Securities.* Princeton: Princeton University Press for National Bureau of Economic Research, 1960.

54. Scott, William A. *Repudiation of State Indebtedness.* New York: Thomas Y. Crowell & Co., 1893.

55. Seiden, Martin H. *The Quality of Trade Credit.* Occasional Paper No. 87. New York: National Bureau of Economic Research, 1964.

56. Shattuck, Leroy A., Jr. *Municipal Indebtedness: A Study of the Debt to Property Ratio.* Baltimore: The Johns Hopkins Press, 1940.

57. Starner, Frances L. *General Obligation Bond Financing by Local Governments: A Survey of State Controls.* Berkeley: University of California Press, 1961.

58. Strudenski, Paul. *Public Borrowing.* New York: National Municipal League, 1930.

59. Trull, Edna. *Resources and Debts of the Forty-Eight States.* New York: Dun & Bradstreet, Inc., 1937.

60. White, J. Austin. *An Analysis of Municipal Bonds.* Cincinnati: J. A. White & Co., 1942.

61. Wojnilower, Albert M. *The Quality of Bank Loans: A Study of Bank*

Examination Records Occasional Paper No. 82. New
York: National Bureau of Economic Research, 1962.

Articles and Periodicals

62. Aronson, J. Richard. "The Idle Cash Balances of State and Local Governments," *Journal of Finance*, XXIII, No. 3 (June 1968), 499-508.

63. *Bank and Quotation Record*. 1928-1969.

64. Bird, Frederick L. "Cities and Their Debt Burden," *National Municipal Review*, XXV, No. 1 (January 1936), 12-19.

65. Bonin, Joseph M. "Principles of State and Local Debt Management," *Municipal Finance*, XXV, No. 3 (February 1963), 121-128.

66. Bond Buyer. *Municipal Financial Statistics* (Vols. I-VII) New York: The Bond Buyer, 1963-1969.

67. Brazier, Harvey E., Suits, Daniel B., and Converse, Muriel W. "Municipal Bond Yields: The Market's Reaction to Michigan's Financial Crisis," *National Tax Journal*, XV, No. 1 (March 1962), 66-70.

68. Brophy, Charles. "State and Local Credit Strengthens Measurably Despite High Bond Sales," *The Daily Bond Buyer*, Special Conference Issue No. 2 (June 20, 1960), 58-68.

69. Brown, J. T. "Early Banking in Mississippi and the Union Bank Bonds," *The Weekly Bond Buyer*, LXXX, No. 3390 (March 29, 1958), 3, 26-29.

70. Chatters, Carl H. "Governmental Defaults – Causes and Prevention: The Problems of Municipal Defaults," *The Daily Bond Buyer* (December 14, 1932), 2039-2040.

71. Chatters, Carl H. "What the Depression Has Done to Municipal Finance," *Public Management*, XVI, No. 12 (December 1934), 383-388.

72. Clark, Charles. "The Case for Municipal Bonds," *Barrons*, XX, No. 31 (July 29, 1940), 18.

73. Carleton, Willard T. and Lerner, Eugene M. "Statistical Credit Scoring of Municipal Bonds." An unpublished research report financed by the Federal Deposit Insurance Corporation.

74. *Commercial and Financial Chronicle*. 1924-1969.

75. *The Daily Bond Buyer*. 1891-1969.

76. Dun and Bradstreet, Inc. Credit reports on numerous state and local bond issues and unpublished summaries of this data.

77. Earley, James S. "The Quality of Credit in Booms and Depressions," *Towards a Firmer Basis of Economic Policy*, Forty-First Annual Report of the National Bureau of Economic Research, New York (1961), 61-66.

78. Eastman Dillion Union Securities & Co. "Rules Under Federal Securities Laws Applicable to 'Industrial Revenue Bonds'."

79. *Federal Reserve Bulletins*. 1948-1969.

80. Goodman, Roy M., Harries, Brenton W., Reilly, James F., and Riehle, Robert C. "Municipal Bond Ratings," *Financial Analysts Journal*, XXIV, No. 3 (May-June 1968), 59-73.

81. Heins, A. James. "The Interest Rate Differential Between Revenue Bonds and General Obligations: A Regression Model," *National Tax Journal*, XV, No. 4 (December 1962), 399-405.

82. Homer, Sidney. "The Changing Market for Municipal Bonds." Special Bulletin 1964A. Chicago: Municipal Finance Officers Association, 1964.

83. *I.B.A. Statistical Bulletin*. (Prepared by the Investment Bankers Association of America, Washington), Nos. 1-33, 1956-1969.

84. Jantscher, Gerald R. "The Effects of Changes in Credit Ratings Upon Municipal Borrowing Costs." An unpublished paper financed by Brookings Institution.

85. Kerekes, Gabe. "The Money Market," *The Weekly Bond Buyer* (published weekly by Goodbody & Co., New York), March 22, 1963.

86. Kurnow, Ernest. "The Nonguaranteed Debt of State and Local Gov-

ernments," *National Tax Journal*, XV, No. 3 (September 1962), 239-245.

87. Lehman, Henry W. "The Federal Municipal Bankruptcy Act," *Journal of Finance*, V, No. 3 (September 1960), 241-256.

88. Lent, George E. "The Origin and Survival of Tax Exempt Securities," *National Tax Journal*, XII, No. 4 (December 1959), 301-316.

89. Linen, John S. "Causes and Effects of Deterioration in Municipal Credit," *National Municipal Review*, XXIII, No. 2 (February 1934), 87-91.

90. *Moody's Municipals and Governments*. (Published semi-weekly by Moody's Investors Service, Inc., New York), 1929-1969.

91. Moore, Geoffrey H. "The Quality of Credit in Booms and Depressions," *The Journal of Business*, XI (May 1956), 288-300.

92. Morris, Frank E. "Impact of Monetary Policy on State and Local Governments: An Empirical Study," *Journal of Finance*, XV, No. 2 (May 1960), 232-249.

93. Netzer, Dick. "State-Local Response to Changing Credit Conditions: The Institutional Obstacles," *Journal of Finance*, XV, No. 2 (May 1960), 221-231.

94. Pico, Rafael. "A New Look at Debt Limits," *Municipal Finance*, XXXV, No. 1 (August 1962), 14-19.

95. Preston, Nathaniel S. "The Bondholder and the Public Authority: Financial Control," *Municipal Finance*, XXXV, No. 3 (February 1963), 129-147.

96. Rand and Company. "Original Offering Scales." Reoffering yields on new state and local bond issues. New York: Rand and Co., 1957-1968.

97. Rightor, C. E. "Financial Planning," *The Municipal Yearbook, 1935*, Prepared by the International City Managers Association, Chicago (1935), 15-21.

98. Rightor, C. E. "The Bonded Debt of 383 Cities as of January 1, 1936," *National Municipal Review*, XXV, No. 6 (June 1936), 354-368.

99. Severson, Harry L. "The Formative Century in the Evolution of To-day's State and Local Bonds." *The Daily Bond Buyer*, Special Conference Issue No. 1 (May 22, 1961), 7-9, 48-57.

100. Shanks, Sanders, Jr. "The Present State of Municipal Credit," *National Municipal Review*, XXIII, No. 2 (February 1934), 92-95.

101. Shanks, Sanders, Jr. "The Extent of Municipal Defaults," *National Municipal Review*, XXIV, No. 1 (January 1935), 32-34.

102. Shanks, Sanders, Jr. "Municipal Bond Defaults," *National Municipal Review*, XXVI, No. 6 (June 1937), 296-298.

103. Smith, Wade S. "What's Ahead for State and Local Finance," *Banking* (October 1961), 4-8.

104. "State and Local Government Borrowing" *Monthly Review* (Federal Reserve Bank of New York), XL, No. 3 (March 1962), 34-39.

105. Tausig, Russell. "Governmental Accounting: Fund Flow or Service Cost," *The Accounting Review*, XXXVIII, No. 3 (July 1963), 562-567.

106. Tyler, Walter H. "Importance of Bond Ratings to Municipal Management," *Alabama Municipal Journal*, XVII, No. 1 (July 1959), 5-7.

107. Tyler, Walter H. "Revenue Bond Financing: Advantages and Disadvantages," *Municipal Finance*, XXXII, No. 1 (August 1959), 76-80.

108. *The Wall Street Journal*. 1926-1969.

109. West, Richard. "New Issue Concessions on Municipal Bonds: A Case of Monopsony Pricing," *Journal of Business*, XXXVIII, No. 2 (April 1965), 135-148.

110. Wonders, George. "State Bond Defaults," *The Daily Bond Buyer*, CLXVIII, No. 20331 (April 16, 1958), 1744, 1764.

111. Wood, David M., Kushell, C. J., Jr., and Mitchell, George W., "Revenue Bond Financing – Legal, Operating, and Economic Aspects," *Journal of Finance*, X, No. 2 (May 1955), 201-233.

112. *The Weekly Bond Buyer*. 1955-1969.

Reports and Public Documents

113. Advisory Commission on Intergovernmental Relations. *State Constitutional and Statutory Restrictions on Local Government Debt.* Commission Report A-10. Washington: Government Printing Office, 1961.

114. Advisory Commission on Intergovernmental Relations. *Directory of Federal Statistics for Metropolitan Areas.* Information Report M18. Washington: Government Printing Office, 1962.

115. Advisory Commission on Intergovernmental Relations. *Measures of State and Local Fiscal Capacity and Tax Effort.* Staff Report M16. Washington: Government Printing Office, 1962.

116. Advisory Commission on Intergovernmental Relations. *State Constitutional and Statutory Restrictions on Local Taxing Powers.* Commission Report A-14. Washington: Government Printing Office, 1962.

117. Anderson, William. *The Units of Government in the United States.* Chicago: Public Administration Service, 1934.

118. Citizens Research Council of Michigan. *Constitutional Earmarking of State Tax Revenues.* Con-Con Research Paper No. 7. Detroit: Citizens Research Council of Michigan, 1962.

119. Joint Economic Committee of U.S. Congress. *State and Local Public Facility Needs and Financing.* Washington: Government Printing Office, 1966.

120. Investment Bankers Association. *Municipal Bond Ratings – 1957-1961.* Occasional Paper No. 3. Washington: Investment Bankers Association, January 1963.

121. Investment Bankers Association. *Regulation Q and Municipal Bond Yields.* Occasional Paper No. 4. Washington: Investment Bankers Association, May 1963.

122. Moody's Investors Service, Inc. *Moody's Municipal and Governments Manuals.* New York: Moody's Investors Service, Inc., 1919-1969.

123. National Association of Supervisors of State Banks. *Municipals.* Report of Committee on Municipal Obligations. Washington: Federal

Deposit Insurance Corp., 1941.

124. New Jersey Commission to Investigate Municipal Taxation and Expenditures. *Municipal and County Data*. Trenton: State of New Jersey, 1931.

125. Standard and Poor's Corporation. *Municipal Bond Selector*. New York: Standard and Poor's Corporation, 1962-1969.

126. Tax Foundation, Inc. *Earmarked State Taxes*. Project Note No. 38. New York: Tax Foundation, Inc., 1964.

127. Tax Foundation, Inc. *Facts and Figures in Government Finance*. Englewood Cliffs, N. J.: Prentice-Hall, Inc., 1955-1969.

128. U.S. Bureau of the Census. *Public Debt*. Washington: Government Printing Office, 1924.

129. U.S. Bureau of the Census. *Financial Statistics of State and Local Governments, 1932*. Washington: Government Printing Office, 1932.

130. U.S. Bureau of the Census. *State and Local Debt: 1941*. Washington: Government Printing Office, 1942.

131. U.S. Bureau of the Census. *County and City Data Book*. A Statistical Abstract Supplement. Washington: Government Printing Office, 1949, 1952, 1956, 1962, and 1967.

132. U.S. Bureau of the Census. *Governmental Finances*. Released Annually. Washington: Government Printing Office, 1952-1968.

133. U.S. Bureau of the Census. *Historical Statistics on State and Local Government Finances, 1902-1953*. Special Study No. 38. Washington: Government Printing Office, 1955.

134. U.S. Bureau of the Census. *Historical Summary of Governmental Finances: Finances in the United States*. Vol. IV, No. 3, 1957 Census of Governments. Washington: Government Printing Office, 1959.

135. U.S. Bureau of the Census. *Taxable Property Values*. Vol. II, 1962 Census of Governments. Washington: Government Printing Office, 1963.

136. U.S. Bureau of the Census. *Compendium of Government Finances*. Vol. IV, No. 4, 1962 Census of Governments. Washington: Government Printing Office, 1964.

137. U.S. Bureau of the Census. *Compendium of Government Finances*. Vol. IV, No. 5, 1967 Census of Governments. Washington: Government Printing Office, 1969.

138. U.S. Census Office. *Report on Valuation, Taxation, and Public Indebtedness*. Vol. VII of the Tenth Census, 1880. Washington: Government Printing Office, 1884.

139. U.S. Chamber of Commerce. *Debt: Public and Private*. Report of the Committee on Economic Policy. Washington: Chamber of Commerce, 1961.

140. U.S. Comptroller of the Currency. *Annual Reports*. Washington: Government Printing Office, 1947-1968.

141. U.S. Department of Commerce. *Wealth, Debt, and Taxation, 1913*. Vol. I.

142. U.S. Department of Commerce. *Indebtedness in the United States, 1929-1941*. Washington: Government Printing Office, 1942.

143. U.S. Department of Commerce. *Survey of Current Business*. Published Monthly. Washington: Government Printing Office, 1945-1969.

144. *U.S. Magazine and Democratic Review*. XII (February 1843), 211-212.

145. U.S. Treasury Department. *Annual Reports of the Secretary of the Treasury on the State of the Finances*. Washington: Government Printing Office, 1946-1968.

Index